THE QUICK AND THE DEAD

By the same author

Against the Stranger: Lives in Occupied Territory

THE QUICK AND THE DEAD

UNDER SIEGE IN SARAJEVO

JANINE DI GIOVANNI

PHOENIX HOUSE

LONDON

First published in Great Britain in 1994
by Phoenix House, Orion House,
5 Upper St Martin's Lane,
London WC2H 9EA

Copyright © 1994 Janine di Giovanni

Grateful acknowledgement is made to the author for permission to quote the line on p 29
from *Tito and the Rise and Fall of Yugoslavia* by Richard West, published by Sinclair
Stevenson. The extract from *Seasons in Hell* by Ed Vulliamy (© Ed Vulliamy 1994) on p 68
is reproduced by kind permission of Simon & Schuster, London. The lines on p 176 are
reproduced by kind permission of Reed Consumer Books from *The Sorrow of War* by Bao
Ninh, published by Secker & Warburg. The lines on p 116 from 'Not Waving But
Drowning' by Stevie Smith are reproduced by kind permission of Virago Press. The lines
on p 15 from 'The Truth the Dead Know' by Anne Sexton are reproduced by kind
permission of Virago Press from *Selected Poems*. The passage by Mikhail Steblin-Kamensky
on p vii is extracted from 'The Siege of Leningrad' which appeared in Granta 30, originally
titled 'The Dragon' (1943) and published in Neva 1, Moscow, in 1989. *Witness to Genocide*
by Roy Gutman is published in the UK by Element Books and in the US by the Macmillan
Publishing Co.

A CIP catalogue record for this book is
available from the British Library

ISBN 1 89758 0 95 9

Filmset by Selwood Systems, Midsomer Norton
Printed in Great Britain by Butler & Tanner, Frome and London

For Jonathan Cooper, with love.
And for my godson, Deni Jovan Jokic.

'The bloody massacre in Bangladesh quickly covered over the memory of the Russian invasion of Czechoslovakia, the assassination of Allende drowned out the groans of Bangladesh, the war in the Sinai Desert made people forget Allende, the Cambodian massacre made people forget the Sinai, and so on and so forth until ultimately everyone lets everything be forgotten.'

Milan Kundera, *The Book of Laughter and Forgetting*
Faber & Faber

'Every time he passed a sled coming in the opposite direction, carrying something wrapped up or wound up like a mummy, Alexander Ivanovich would glance at it with curiosity; it always turned out to be what he thought it was. He counted fourteen sleds before he reached home. One corpse was being carried on a child's pram, which bumped and jolted along the ruts in the road. And the living people coming towards him walked like corpses, if corpses could walk; they clutched walking-sticks in outstretched hands; their bodies were bent as though their centre of gravity had moved somewhere higher than usual; their faces had no expression.'

Mikhail Steblin-Kamensky, *The Siege of Leningrad*

CONTENTS

ACKNOWLEDGEMENTS

IN BOSNIA: the Susko family, Mario, Marija, Sandra; Klea and Zoran Jokic; Dr Vesna, Nino and Mama Cegnic, Dragan Klajanc, Dina and Edin Hamzic; Dina 'Three Sugars' AFP; Samir, Amra, Elma and Sabina from Reuters; Cile, Zaim and Talijan from BH High Command, Colonel Jovan Divjak, Zlatko Zelic; Gordana Knezevic, Dr Ejup Ganic; Nadja, Bojen, Dada Hadzihalilovic; Senada Kreso; Jasmina; in Zagreb, Vesna Klanac; in Mostar: Robert and Orhan and Alma and Arif Pasalic; Armand Bratonic and his family; the staff at Radio Mostar. And to all the staff of the Holiday Inn, in particular Suad Podrug, Amira Dealic and Sead Boric. At the UNHCR, Peter Kessler.

Also, my colleagues: Kurt Schork and Corinne Dufka of Reuters; Ariane Quentier of RTL; Patrick Bishop of the *Daily Telegraph*; Renzo Cianfanelli of *Corriere della Sera*; Joel Brand of *Newsweek*; Didier François of Libération; Jean-Marie Le Maire; Ed Vulliamy; Ian Traynor of the *Guardian*; ABC News, in particular Carlo Brierelli and Gordon in Split; Bruno Silvester and Fiona Turner, ABC, CBS News for their kindness in shipping my satellite phone; Roy Gutman of *New York Newsday*; John Burns of the *New York Times*; Barry and Charley in EBU; Paul Lowe of Magnum; Gary Knight of SABA; Tom Stoddart; Nicky Millard and Matt from Newsforce; David Mills and Jeremy Bowen; Alan Little, Martin Dawes of the BBC; Roger Hutchings of Network; Chris Helgren of Reuters; Andrew and Atka Reid;

Jonathan Landy of the *Christian Science Monitor*; Enrico Dagnino, Ron Haviv, Jon Jones, Philippe Simon of RMC.

Also, Bimba da Maria of RAI; Anna Maria Tremonti and Mike Grippo of CBC; Shelley Saywell of Binashi Films; Karen Lajon of JDD; Bob Reid, Peter Northall, Samir and Terry Leonard of AP; Kevin Sullivan, Marija and Jamal of UPI; Penny Marshall of ITN; the staff of *Oslobodenje* and in particular, Senad Gubelic.

At the *Sunday Times*: Sue Douglas and Andrew Neil encouraged me throughout the war, Tony Rennell, John Witherow, Bob Tyrer, Tony Bambridge and Kate Carr. Sian Roberts, Sally McKenna, Clare Istead, Kathleen Heron and Angela Ponnel.

Finally, David Godwin spent hours coaxing me into writing, Maggie McKernan and Nick McDowell brought the book to print.

Janine di Giovanni
London
July 1994

INTRODUCTION

THERE IS A VERY SIMPLE THEORY about war, that it brings out the best and the worst in people. In any given city, at any given time, if you have war, you have dichotomy: those who make money from war and those who lose everything. Life and death, good and evil, heroes and freaks, angels and devils.

The siege of Sarajevo officially began on 6 April 1992, but to most people it began on the day they realised they could not leave the city, that borders were sealed and they were trapped forever in a valley surrounded by mountains and guns. What happened inside that city is what this book is about – the people who lived there, the people who left, the emotions, the reality of survival in Sarajevo.

At the start of the war – quickly described in the West as a civil war, although anyone who watched the bombardment of Sarajevo knew that it was a war of aggression – all the men of fighting age were quickly rounded up and sent to the front lines. Most of them had not held a gun since their military training years before, but as Roy Gutman, the *New York Newsday* journalist who won a Pulitzer for his reporting in Bosnia remarked in his book, *Witness to Genocide*:

Militarily, Bosnia-Hercegovina could hardly have been worse off. Bosnia's Muslims were not the fierce Mujahedin warriors of Serb propaganda; they were mostly city dwellers, artisans,

I

teachers, doctors, small businessmen and farmers, predominantly pacifists. Women do not wear the chador, men rarely wear a fez or attend religious services; Muslims in Bosnia viewed their religion as a national identity and saw themselves as secular Europeans first, Muslims second ... they did not have an army, a military tradition or weapons ... from the outside it looked like a hopeless case, but principles were at stake, as was the existence of a European nation.

The people of Sarajevo were not fighters, nor were the Muslims of Sarajevo mujahedin, as the Serbs later tried to portray them: before the war, attendance in the mosques was about 3 per cent. Everything they learned about warfare came from their two-year military service and the basic instinct to survive and defend their city. As Gutman later points out, people fighting for their lives, their families and their land are highly motivated, however poorly armed. And because the war in Sarajevo was an urban one, because neighbourhoods and areas were specifically targeted and militias (schoolfriends, really) would band together to hold the territory, it became a war that focused more on civilians than on land.

'Imagine, one day you are sitting in London,' one of my friends a Serb who had remained in the city and fought on the Bosnian side, said to me one day, 'and the barricades go up, and you start getting attacked by the Welsh, or the Scots. Imagine that suddenly your water is turned off, your electricity, and your brothers, your father, your boyfriend are sent off to the front line to become snipers. They don't come back. Your city is destroyed, and Europe looks on and does nothing. What would happen to you inside?'

Something happened inside all of us who reported the war in Sarajevo on a long-term, consistent basis, because Sarajevo was an emotional story. Despite the endless diplomatic dithering, the broken ceasefires, the days and weeks spent waiting for air strikes, and the belief that hope was slowly filtering out of the place as the West refused to act. It was difficult to be just an observer, unable to make or affect policy, facing friends and families in Sarajevo who constantly asked for help. The only way to channel the anger and, at times, the bitterness was to report what was happening inside the city and hope that someone was reading it.

Inside the city, people went on trying to live, trying to believe that someone outside was aware of what was happening. When Radio Zid (Wall), Sarajevo's alternative station, was set up in January 1993, its founder, Zdravko Grebo, distributed this manifesto:

You must have seen more than once the images of devastated and massacred Bosnia-Hercegovina, and among these the singularly horrifying images of Sarajevo. But what could not be recognised in those images was the slaughtering of the civic spirit and culture of the country's urban parts. The demolished buildings, collapsed bridges and other edifices will be restored, more easily than the urban and civilisational spirit that had been created over the centuries ...

... why the name Radio Sarajevo Zid? Not long ago, there was a town divided by a wall. The wall was toppled down and millions around the globe thought that the world had come a step closer to Utopia. Then the war in Bosnia-Hercegovina started. Sarajevo is not divided by a wall, Sarajevo is divided by hatred. Nationalistic fanaticism and madness emanate from people that have never been Sarajevans, who have never been civilians. This whole city, together with other Bosnian-Hercegovinan towns, has become a wall. The wall in front of which the conscience and morale of the world's mighty ones is stopped, unable to cross.

Sarajevo felt forgotten during those terrible days when hundreds of shells fell, and the air was thick with that smell of mortars. But there were also emotional moments of great inspiration and courage. Perhaps because the intensity of that day-to-day living is so high, you very quickly develop extraordinary bonds with people.

I met Professor Mario Susko under the most unusual circumstances. In December 1992, I was sitting on a table in an office in the old Sarajevo city hall building, then called the International Peace Centre, and a man called Ibrahim was making a drawing of my foot. In his old life, that is, his life before the war, he had been a shoemaker and he said he used to make beautiful Italian shoes with heels; he said it would give him pleasure to try to make a pair for me. It was two weeks before Christmas in that first year of war and he was tracing the outline of my sole onto a piece of cardboard. I was protesting quietly, deeply embarrassed about having my foot drawn in the middle of a war, when the door opened and a small man with a beard entered, bowing slightly. He had thick glasses and a twitch; he shook my hand and in perfect English with a New York accent, said, 'Do you have a cigarette?'

I gave him one of my Marlboros, from the stash I had bought in Kiseljak, the border town on the outskirts of Sarajevo, and lit it for him. His hand shook gratefully, his voice rasped. He said that he had come to find me because he heard I was looking for a family to spend Christmas with – a Catholic Croat family whose lives had been destroyed by the war. He invited me to his home to meet his wife and daughters. 'But it's not really my home,' he said nervously, his eyes flickering across the room. 'My home was burnt down in Dobrinja.' Dobrinja is a suburb that was under fire, a siege within a siege, during the summer.

That was the beginning. The Suskos would go on to play a

major role in my life over the next two years. We did not know then what would happen – that they would leave Sarajevo, go to England, to America, that their family unit would be ripped apart, that they would leave everything they had behind. That afternoon in Sarajevo, December 1992, we arranged to meet the next day in a place that was not exposed to snipers, and our friendship began.

Now it is June 1994, two years after the destruction of the city began, and I am poring through nearly two years of notebooks, of words and incidents and moments that I had nearly forgotten – or perhaps tried very hard to forget, because at times they were so terrible. There are notes from press briefings, conversations with politicians, artists, writers, soldiers, and my own diaries. There are accounts of days on the front lines, but also of parties and, oddly enough, incredible moments – when my godson, Mario's grandson Deni, was baptised on a beautiful spring day in Sarajevo cathedral; when the first café opened; a party given by some artist friends of mine who had recently married; or the feeling on Christmas Eve when I heard the sound of voices raised in song in a church on Snipers' Alley.

Today, I am preparing to return to Sarajevo for the first time in nearly two and a half months, the longest time I have been away from Bosnia. I am packing the usual things, but wondering whether or not it is necessary to take my helmet, and removing the ceramic plates from my flak jacket. That kind of thing would have been unthinkable a year ago, but since the February NATO ultimatum, when the Serbs grudgingly pulled back some of their heavy artillery from the hills above Sarajevo, the snipers have been quiet. My friends told me that the 'Pazi Snajper' (Warning Sniper!) signs that used to hang on the more dangerous streets have been removed, that the Run or RIP sign outside the Holiday Inn has been removed, and that it was possible, for a few weeks in the summer, to walk down Snipers' Alley, and to walk, instead of run, between gaps in buildings. There are traffic lights working in the streets – a bizarre, surreal thought in a city that did not have electricity for so long – and meat for sale in the covered market off Marsala Tito street.

But how can you recover from a siege mentality? Is it possible for Sarajevo to forget, to recover, or just return to a normal life, the sort of things that all of us take for granted but that the people there have been denied. I remember a friend from Sarajevo being fixated at Zagreb airport, turning on a tap of water, because the taps in Sarajevo were dry. And picking up a telephone that was not connected to a satellite for $40 a minute. In Sarajevo the telephone lines were cut shortly after the war began.

Now, I have just picked up the phone and dialled 387 – the code for Bosnia – and 71 – for Sarajevo – and the telephone number of my friend, Dr Vesna Cegnic. She is a surgeon at the State Hospital in Sarajevo, a doctor who worked despite the fact that her hospital was being deliberately targeted, and who had to administer medicine and try to save lives in medieval conditions. I cannot believe it when she answers the phone and tells me, half laughing, half crying, that this is the first phone call she has had from outside Sarajevo in two years. 'It's almost normal here,' she says. 'Sugar is only 25 DM a pound – can you believe it! The sun is shining! The trams are running! And the phone is working! I love you!'

I remember Gordana Knezevic, the deputy editor of *Oslobodenje*, the Sarajevo daily that came out every day of the war, remarking, on a freezing cold winter day as she sat in her flat wearing a hat and wrapped in a shawl, that it would not take very long to become acclimatised to a normal life again. 'All I want,' she said dreamily, 'is to sit outside on a Sunday afternoon, in the garden with the children, and read the newspapers without being frightened of a shell coming in.' Such a small thing to

6

want, but it was those minute details of ordinary life that had been denied, and that drove people to the point of near madness. As one psychiatrist from Kosevo hospital remarked, Sarajevo at times resembled a walking lunatic asylum – the effects of the war were so great that she believed nearly 90 per cent of the population would suffer from some sort of post-traumatic stress long after the final ceasefire was installed, the papers signed, and Bosnia torn apart by what the United Nations refer to as the warring factions. I cannot believe Sarajevo is again nearly a normal town, because for so long it was surreal, like living in the twilight zone.

Someone I met in Sarajevo on one of my first trips there remarked that Yugoslavia was like a wind tunnel, sucking everything around it back in time, the century beginning and ending with a brutal and vicious conflict. It is impossible to count the dead, or in fact the living, but the war in the former Yugoslavia is reckoned to have killed roughly 200,000 people and to have created nearly 3 million refugees. During the post-World War II period in Bosnia, more than one in four marriages were mixed. It is not a civil war, nor a war against Muslims because, as they will repeatedly tell you, they are not Muslims but Bosnians. It is not a war against Islam, but a war against civilians, against humanity.

This book does not centre on the breakup of Yugoslavia, the war in Croatia, or even the war in Central Bosnia, aside from a chapter on Mostar and some memories of the last days of Jajce, the refugees in Travnik and the siege of Maglaj. It is a personal memoir, an attempt not to forget, an attempt to remember what those days were like, how people lived, how they died.

THE DEAD

WINTER 1992

THEY SAID IT WAS a mild winter by Sarajevo standards but that first winter of the war it was so cold that people kept dying in their sleep. The worst night of the winter came a few days after New Year when ten old people who were living in an abandoned nursing home on the front line went to sleep wrapped in a few icy, filthy blankets and never woke up. Ten died in three days and there was no one to remove the bodies because most of the staff had run away from the shelling and the constant shooting of a sniper who was positioned in a house about 25 metres away. That week, the temperature dropped to 15 below zero and the skin on the back of my legs was so dry and chapped it began to peel when I took off the three layers of clothes that I wore.

The nursing home, ironically called the Centre for the Protection of Old People, was situated between two front lines – Bosnian Serb and Bosnian Muslim – and except for the occasional French UN soldier who passed through, or the UNHCR who sometimes brought plastic for the windows which had been blown away, it had been forgotten. The few members of staff who had stayed despite the sniper had to cook, chop wood, clean the emaciated bodies that were still alive, and wrap and bury the dead.

There were some neighbours left in the surrounding farmhouses – no one was quite sure why they had not run away during the last battle, but sometimes people refused to leave their houses. Instead, they would lock themselves in with their redundant television sets, their photographs, their china, as though those inanimate objects could act as talismans to protect them from what was going on outside their door. They would rather be burned out or shelled or rounded up and taken off to some camp than desert their houses, their last link with reality, with normality, with a life before the war.

Sometimes, you would catch glimpses of that life: going for coffee in someone's house, they would use their last spoonful of beans, saved from the day before the war, and serve it in their best cups. Once, in Maglaj, I found a wedding photograph lying in a heap of glass after a mortar attack, and on the road to Nedzarici, there was a rug hanging on a fence outside a house now manned by Serbian soldiers. I remember that rug because it was beautiful, red and gold, old Turkish, probably once in someone's dining room, and now stiff with ice and mud and rain. Someone had left it behind before abandoning that house, and no one had stolen it because unlike milk or cigarettes or whisky or coffee, it had no value.

The story of the nursing home remained relatively unreported for some time. Then, someone brave wandered across a barren field to the Holiday Inn, the hotel where the journalists stayed, because something horrific was happening and they had to find a reporter because no one else – not the UN, not the War Government, not even their families – would listen. Those people were not afraid to walk to the hotel, which was in one of the most exposed (everything in Sarajevo during the worst days was evaluated as either exposed or protected) neighbourhoods. They could not come through the front entrance on Snipers' Alley – only a fool would walk on the side facing the Parliament building, directly in line with the snipers – nor through the side entrance, which was gutted by anti-tank rounds. They must have crossed the field across from the Unis Towers, twin buildings with entire floors burned away. Then they would have run through the field littered with weeds and car parts and broken glass and through the bullet-riddled back door.

Someone came that day and told the Reuters office on the fifth floor about the people in Nedzarici, and we drove out, in an armoured car, skidding on the heavy snow which had fallen the night before. In the whiteness, Sarajevo was transformed: suddenly the blackened buildings appeared white, their shell holes filled, the burnt-out decay from the fires the previous summer painted over by the snow. Even the sound of artillery fire seemed muffled, fainter, as though it was coming not from the hills above the city where people used to ski at weekends, but from far away.

Nedzarici, a Serb-held suburb out near the airport, was a dangerous trip to make because it involved driving first down Snipers' Alley, turning left onto the airport ramp, passing the United Nations checkpoint and two front lines before you reached the home. Crowded in the cab of the armoured car, we felt safer, although anti-aircraft or anti-tank rounds could puncture the armour like a knife going through paper. A BBC cameraman had been killed on the road near Turbe the autumn before. He was getting one last shot of refugees staggering down the road. Someone who saw it, who was in the car behind him, said it happened so quickly, the burst of light and then the explosions, and then the instant death, and it made everyone who ever reported in Bosnia realise that there was no logic to when the trigger was pulled, and that uncertainty was part of the fear.

The road to Nedzarici was gutted with shell holes. The Land Rover swerved to avoid some soldiers, Serbs in blue and grey uniforms with arm patches and guns slung over their shoulders,

walking down the road towards a farmhouse that had been
turned into a Serbian command. We stopped briefly, spoke to
one of the two toothless guards that ran the command, and then
drove down the small stretch of exposed road, parked the car
and ran quickly, Indian file, into the house. The day before a 78-
year-old man had been shot between the eyes. He had been
chopping wood, trying to keep the place warm. The Reuters
correspondent went first, I went second, thinking as I ran about
all those relay races I lost when I was a kid. A carload of French
journalists who had followed went after me. Inside, near the
entrance, was an old man, standing motionless, watching us
quietly. He raised his hand in a kind of greeting, but when the
sniper shot, he did not flinch, even his eyes did not register the
sound of the gun. I had seen the same thing happen with small
children: they did not move when they heard the whistle of a
mortar or the sound of a sniper round because they had become
so used to it.

The interior of the home had been almost completely
destroyed by shelling. Shreds of wood, shards of glass, broken
bricks, useless furniture, beds, chairs, seared blankets were thrown
into a heap in the centre. It was so cold our breath came out in
icy clouds, but you could still smell the burning from the shelling,
and there was a worse, more fetid smell. Off to the left was a
military-style kitchen; on a wood stove, a pot of water was
boiling with some beans.

A cat with a broken leg limped past the pile of rubbish. The
old man from the entrance shuffled slowly over and pointed to
the blown-out windows lining the hallway. 'Snayper,' he croaked.
Sniper. The strangest thing, perhaps the hardest and most surreal
thing to comprehend about a war which focuses on civilians, is
that you are never really safe, not in a building, not in your own
home. Three of us ran down a hallway with windows on one
side, and only stopped running when we got to a series of rooms

that weren't exposed to the sniper. These were the bedrooms of the dead.

There were three rooms. Seven women and three men, dead for several hours, all of them wrapped in blankets, soiled, all of them already stiff with rigor mortis and the cold. The smell of shit and death was unbearable, and I wrapped the wool scarf I had bought in Zagreb around my face. A French reporter came up behind me and pulled it away. We stood quietly, and then he went into the next room.

The bodies were pathetically small, or so they seemed, lying on the floor with only their swollen feet in holey woollen socks sticking out. Their mouths were open, their skin had become waxen. Perhaps, before the war or time had reduced them to a bundle on the floor of a destroyed building in the middle of a front line, they had been people's children, parents, wives, husbands, but now they were nothing more than piles of skin and bones, faceless, nameless.

A few people had stayed with the old people, unable to leave them, even as the shelling got worse. One of them was a 40-year-old Croatian psychologist called Lidia Grozinko, whose only daughter was living in Croatia. As everyone else shuffled out and went to find another room, Lidia stayed with me. I could not imagine what it was like to go to sleep, huddled in the only blanket you were allocated, and to freeze to death. I could not take my eyes from their feet, so frozen and vulnerable, and I thought of the poem by Anne Sexton, 'The Truth the Dead Know':

And what of the dead? They lie without shoes
in their stone boats. They are more like stone
than the sea would be if it stopped. They refuse
to be blessed, throat, eye and knucklebone.

I thought about other bodies I had seen, in the hospitals and morgues: the child in the subterranean basement in Travnik hospital whose gut was ripped to shreds by shrapnel as his family tried to escape the fighting near Novi Travnik. I visited him every day, as he lay on some filthy cot, alone because he had been separated from his father, dying in agony because there were no painkillers. A few days later, there was another body: a young Croatian cameraman who was working for the BBC, filming refugees from Jajce after the city fell. He was getting one last shot when his armoured car was pierced by an anti-tank round, and the body was brought to the headquarters near Turbe where I was waiting for a break in the shelling to get back to Travnik. A few hours before he had been alive; now no one knew who he was, or who the blood-spattered camera belonged to. We searched through his kit for some identification; it was all covered with gristle and bone and fresh blood, and his helmet and film containers were sodden. His body was wrapped in a sheet with his feet sticking out. You think the strangest thoughts at times like that: why is he not wearing any shoes? why are his socks pink?

That day in Nedzarici, I opened a door to another room and found more dead bodies and more stained beds. Here they slept six or eight to a room and the ones who had died had not yet been wrapped and moved to the floor. In one corner there were beds piled with old clothing. I walked to one with what I thought was a heap of clothes dumped on top and bent over it. Just then a tiny arm, no bigger than a child's, reached up and grabbed my hand with the last surge of strength in the body. It was not a pile of clothes, but an ancient woman who was still alive, a pale woman with enormous lavender eyes and broken teeth. Her skin was translucent with the cold; she did not have enough calories in her system to concentrate, she could barely focus on my face.

'*Ingleski*,' I whispered to her because I knew she was frightened. '*Novinare Ingleski*.' English journalist.

Her eyes suddenly became lucid. She dug her overgrown yellow nails into my skin and fell back onto the filthy pillow.

'*Zima, zima*,' she whispered back. Her lips were so chapped it was difficult for her to form the words. Cold, cold. Then she pulled the covers over her head. I watched her for a minute more, tucked the blanket around her and left. When I turned back at the door, she looked again like a pile of clothes.

Outside, Lidia was crying. 'I can't think because of the cold,' she said. She had been living at the home for eight months, negotiating with the Serbs for small provisions: some food, a cook and a little money (in Serbian dinars, utterly useless) for the staff. Before the war, there were over 100 workers in the home, taking care of 108 people. Now there were six − a psychologist, a social worker and four people to clean and cook the watery soup and try to find wood. In the past few weeks, the UN, in particular the French battalion at the airport, had brought eight heaters without fuel, soap (there was no water to wash) and cheese.

Lidia was close to breaking point. 'No doctor, no stoves, no wood, everyone gone because of the sniper . . . and every one of those people, those poor people, died from the cold,' she said, moving in between the bodies, touching the wrappings gently. She wiped her nose on the sleeve of her coat.

One staff member who did stay used to make the run in the morning to the bakery off Snipers' Alley, when it was functioning, to get bread. But the day before he had crashed his car, trying to avoid the sniper. His car had been full of dead bodies; he was trying to bring them to Vlakovo, the mixed cemetery for Muslims, Croats and Serbs. 'I am hoping the UN will give us a new car,' she said. Someone, one of the journalists in the room, laughed cynically and Lidia heard him. 'I know. I know what you are thinking,' she said quietly. 'Five months ago I wrote a letter to the headquarters warning that this might happen.' The UN replied that they could evacuate, but could not make a decision about where to place the old people.

They all died early in the morning, at dawn when it was coldest, and Lidia thought they knew when they were dying. After struggling for days with the intense cold, some simply gave up. One 72-year-old woman, Katica Getlig, told Lidia before she pulled the covers over her face that she would be dead by morning. 'Thank you for everything you did,' she whispered. When Lidia checked on her a few hours later, dragging herself up in the cold to make the rounds of the freezing rooms by herself, Katica was dead. 'What could I possibly do? At least she died quickly.'

It seemed worse to live. They had no light in the evenings, it got dark at 4 pm, only a few candles made from oil and wick floating in a glass. Or they sat in the darkness, sometimes talking, sometimes silent. They slept six or eight to a room. They lived on tea for breakfast and dinner, some rice, some cabbage broth boiled with a few bones. They waited for water from the UN. 'There are twenty generators sitting in the parking lot of UNPROFOR,' Lidia said sardonically. 'Instead of using them, we are freezing to death.'

When wood could be found they would huddle together in one room at the top of the house, around a single wood stove, one of the three wood stoves in the house. They were washed once a month, if they were lucky once every fifteen days. There was no water, no lavatories, no way of washing the soiled sheets. Lidia pulled a letter from her pocket, written on the 14 August 1992:

TO: UNHCR And UNPROFOR
Please help protect these old people, they are helpless, homeless and sick. They are not guilty for the war.

She was standing with the letter in her hand when the Serb soldier arrived. I was in a room by myself when I heard the shouts, came out, and saw him waving his gun at her. She was speaking quietly, rubbing her hands as she spoke to keep them warm. He motioned us away with his gun. Lidia turned, a look of absolute defeat on her face: 'Okay, you have to go. Go now. Run. Quickly.' I put my hands over my ears as I ran to the Land Rover, thinking of the old man shot between the eyes chopping wood, and wondered what it is that makes a sniper decide to shoot. Why him? Why not me? We left the bodies and drove away from Nedzarici.

Ten minutes away by car, in the former PTT building now used as the UN headquarters in Sarajevo, Jose Marija Mendiluce, director of the UNHCR in Zagreb, calmly listened to the story. At first he appeared surprised and shocked, but then he turned the case over to Mik Magnusson, the Civil Affairs officer, and Barry Frewer, the Canadian commander who ran the morning press briefings. Frewer called a briefing, stumbling slightly over his words. 'The fact that an old people's home exists on a front line is deplorable,' he began, and he went on to address issues as if they were on a checklist: burying the dead, getting stoves, supplies, getting the French battalion to bring blankets. 'We recognise it's a sad, sad situation. But officially there is nothing we can do. We are constantly up against local commanders. The only people who suffer are the local populations.'

Someone asked the obvious: and what are you going to do?

Frewer said, 'This is what one sees in a city under siege where there is no heat, and buildings are blown to pieces and people try to shelter behind plastic windows.' It was a horrendous situation, he said, and we must give peace a chance.

We left. Early the next morning, as more snow came down and the temperature dropped further, some French soldiers went to the home with wood stoves, but neglected to bring an essential tube needed to install them. On 5 January, several days after the first bodies were found, UNPROFOR issued a statement:

> It has been brought to our attention that the situation facing the elderly in an old people's home in the Sarajevo district of Nedzarici is currently under scrutiny ...
>
> The fact that an old people's home exists close to the frontline in a conflict situation is deplorable in itself ... the home was on the list of recipients for aid; stoves and heating fuel were ordered some time ago, but only now are arriving ...
>
> Given the war situation and the difficulty of arranging localised ceasefires it had been hoped that the home could have been evacuated under the auspices of the 13 December agreement reached at the Mixed Military Group ... unfortunately the agreement was not implemented due to the reluctance of one of the parties concerned ...
>
> The UNHCR has been actively pursuing discussions with liaison officers from both the Presidency and Serb sides to find accommodation for the occupants of the home. It should be noted that in this regard this is, as usual, dependent on the parties involved in the civil war ...
>
> The issue of removal of deceased for proper burial has just been brought to our attention. We are examining how we may be of immediate assistance in this matter.

But the words meant nothing because more people died and the Serbs stopped allowing access to the road to Nedzarici. Lidia, on her own, tried to keep track of the dead, but most of the records were lost in the shelling. Who were they? It was impossible to imagine them ever walking, having conversations, ever living. One of them, before the war, had been a well-known opera singer. Another was the 65-year-old uncle of Juka, one of Sarajevo's most famous warlords. Lidia thought that the oldest of the bodies was 72. His name was Riva, a Muslim, he had come from

Sarajevo before the war. The youngest was 57, a Serb, Lidia thought. She smiled wryly. 'But does it matter? You see, in death, there is no war, no Muslims, no Serbs, no Croats. They all die the same way.'

★

Sarajevo, winter 1992, many of the living are also dead.

The city at first appears deserted because there are no cars on the street. In the open-air market off Marsala Tito Street, all but a few tables are empty, covered in snow and a pathetic selection of things for sale: a withered carrot; a pair of dirty mittens; a carton of Marlboros stolen from the UNPROFOR store, selling for 150 DM. A few LPs that can't be played because there is no electricity; a bottle of homemade slivovitz.

And the people moving quickly through the market because it is a dangerous place, frequently shelled, are more like pale ghosts than people. They move without talking, running across intersections and gaps between buildings that are known targets. There is no time to linger, to kiss a friend, because even a second can be risky, the difference between living and dying: if he, or she, had just moved a little faster, they would have been inside when that shell exploded.

And so there is this constant terror, not knowing where, how, when it might land. Inside the one room that he shared with his seventeen-year-old daughter, his wife Marija, his precious dog Sunny and the few books that he managed to bring with him after his apartment in Dobrinja was bombed, Dr Mario Susko, former professor of English Literature at Sarajevo University, has rituals. There is the morning ritual, when he wakes at dawn, in the freezing half light, and lies on his pallet on the floor, listening to the sound of the mortars. Morning is worst, the time when most of the battles in the hills around Sarajevo are at their height, when most of the dead are being carried down the hills in makeshift ambulances, or on the backs of their friends. His 24-year-old son-in-law, Zoran, is on the front line, running with an injured foot. Most of his neighbours, his students, even the younger ones whom he taught rudimentary English in the days before the war, are in the trenches.

It all seems unreal now: but think. Remember what it was like before, when he had a three-bedroomed apartment in Dob-rinja, one of the modern, yuppie ones that were built during the Olympics for the press to stay in. An enormous apartment with wooden fixtures and a terrace and bookshelves crammed with Philip Roth, Seamus Heaney and Saul Bellow and his own notebooks of poetry, translations, lectures. It seems inconceivable, entirely inconceivable, that he once had a life, 52 years of normal life. That he woke up, drove to work, had coffee with students, fell in love, wrote, travelled, dreamed about the days when . . .

I had so many friends, and where are they all now? He is thinking about this as he lies in his bed on the hard floor, covered with a patched blanket, listening to the sounds of the city around him. Sarajevo, December 1992. Eight months into the war, eight months since he has seen a tomato, eaten an egg, had a glass of wine. He's running out of pipe tobacco and dog biscuits. He's got a few left from his last trip to England. Was it only eight months ago that he was living in Norwich, going for long walks around the pond, one month before the war began? Spending his days in the library, translating Seamus Heaney into Serbo-Croat. Or does one say Bosnian now? Before, he had thought of himself as a Catholic Croat, his wife is half-Serb, his two daughters are mixed. Now, since the referendum in April 1991, everyone calls themselves Bosnian.

It seems like light years away, that normal life. In March 1991, Mario Susko was a full professor of English at Sarajevo University.

He was in Norfolk, at the University of East Anglia, when someone sent him a letter describing the government barricades going up around the town, and the sense of tension. He left England on 2 April, and two days later found himself trapped outside the city. 'It was more than a shock for me,' he says. 'I used to take walks, long, long walks around that lake in Norfolk ... and to go from the peace, the green of England to this city that was suddenly at war ... It takes a big psychological leap to get used to that.'

But he came home because he had to. His wife was here, his children. And his city.

Marija is waking slowly, opening her eyes, closing them because she cannot face another day. Then she is rising, rubbing her eyes with her beautiful hands, now scarred from chopping wood in the cellar of her cousin's house where they have a room at the top. Chopping wood, like everything else in her life now, is something that last year, when she worked as a dental technician and met her friends for lunch every day, just to gossip, to laugh, to talk, is something that she could not conceive of doing. She had never chopped wood before. She was the wife of a distinguished professor, the mother of two beautiful daughters, one of them born in America, where they lived for seven years. New York ... 24 years married and always a good life. Now, she can't remember what New York, even Zagreb, looks like; all she can see is the dark skyline of Sarajevo outside the plastic window.

Breakfast is tea left over from Mario's last trip to England. Getting down to the last bits and she is beginning to panic, because there is no tea, no coffee in the city, and the two things Bosnians cannot live without are coffee and tobacco. There is no milk – she cannot remember the last time she had milk – and no bread yet. She is about to pull on her layers and layers of clothes and the boots she wore in the mountains above the city during winter holidays (where the Serb gunners now point their guns – hard to believe that they are the same hills) and she will stand in the long, long bread queue at the one functioning kitchen in the neighbourhood to get a loaf for the entire family. Some days, Marija stands for four, five hours, and gets to the head of the queue and there is none left. Remember croissants for breakfast? Remember biscuits? It all seems like a dream.

She sighs, pulls on her woolly hat, another scarf and leaves the room where Mario is slowly waking up. They feed Sunny his usual diet, rice or macaroni. 6 am.

It's Christmas week, and he's a Catholic, but he's afraid to walk the half mile down the hill from the room where he now lives to go to mass because he's terrified of everything outside: of the nameless gunners in the hills, of the mortars that fall when least expected, of the sniper bullets that rip through kneecaps, hands, throats. At the beginning of the war, his daughter Klea was walking with her baby Deni to stand in the water queue when a bullet ripped through her baggy jeans, searing them but leaving her untouched. She stopped going out after that, but she's still got the jeans and sometimes she takes them out and touches the bullet hole and thinks, they didn't get me.

There are some parts of town Mario will still visit, but only with dread: walking quickly, taking a specific route that has been tested and isn't exposed to snipers, he'll make the journey to the Law School or the Peace Centre in the old city hall building but with a pounding heart. He'll go there, but there are many other parts of town, many streets that he will not go near. Mario has had two close calls which he can't talk about without shaking. The first: 5 June 1992. He'd been in the basement for three days while the shelling got closer and closer to their flat, and despite Marija's protests, he went upstairs to check the damage. He was in the hallway when he saw a 64 mm projectile, a rifle grenade, rip through the kitchen wall. He was in the hallway and suddenly, for eight seconds he was in hell: glass, bricks, concrete, scattered around him. He could see the sky through the hole in the apartment. When he freed himself, he ran downstairs to the basement where Marija and Sandra were huddled in some corner with neighbours and he heard himself screaming, 'Marija, Marija, we have lost our apartment.' He was crying, but only realised when he got downstairs that his face was neatly cut by glass and blood was running down his shirt.

In another life, another time, he would have been preparing exams for his students but instead the battle of Dobrinja, of his neighbourhood, his street, was taking place outside his window. The Bosnian Muslims were, for all practical purposes, defending the city, and the Bosnian Serbs wanted Dobrinja because it was a strategic chunk of land that could effectively split Sarajevo in two. The Bosnians were crippled by an arms embargo imposed by the West, and so Sarajevo was taking 180 mortars for every one it was able to fire. They were sending out their pathetic rounds, trying to fight the weapons of the former Yugoslavian National Army, Europe's third largest force, and the Serbs were pummelling Dobrinja with anti-aircraft rounds that tore into apartment buildings and wiped out two, three, four or five families, entire floors of apartment blocks at a single go, with anti-tank rounds lighting up the buildings like fireworks, with machine guns . . . and snipers, positioned in windows, the most frightening of all.

One month later and the family had moved permanently to the basement. Half of the apartment was gone to rubble and dust, the other half looted. Marija tried to take some clothes, some books, some photographs, but ended up leaving most of it behind. Sandra, sorting through the remains of their life, saw her white ski jacket, the one she had worn the winter before in Jahorina, where the Olympics took place. She stared at it, fingering the silky material, and burst into tears because she had to leave it behind: everyone knows it is far too dangerous to wear a white jacket, an easy target for a sniper.

If May and June meant holding your breath to make the 50-metre dash for humanitarian aid packages, July meant living in the basement like a rat. Marija wept constantly, with fear and exhaustion; Mario sat dumbly staring at a wall. Their biggest fear was for Sandra. At seventeen, she was tall, lithe and beautiful with long honey-coloured hair and enormous blue eyes. She'd lost 30 pounds since the war began, her jeans hung on her, and she hadn't been to school since March 1992: just stopped her life, stopped her studies as though some clock had frozen forever. Then, there was an older boyfriend; and so Sandra was sophisticated and smart, but she was going mad inside the basement wondering if her friends were alive or dead. She was scared of being raped, of what would happen if the Chetniks moved across that 50 metres of land that her schoolfriends were desperately trying to defend. What would happen to her? For weeks, the neighbours had been crowding together telling stories: about the camps in Central Bosnia where Muslims were rounded up like sheep, as the Jews had been in World War II, sent off to be starved and tortured. There was worse, like the stories of Serbs raping women.

At the beginning of August they left Dobrinja, left the basement of their old home, their old life, riding into Sarajevo with the Bosnian Special Police who had been trying to evacuate the few surviving families. Mario took two books with him: an anthology of Bosnian history and a book of his own poems. The notes that he was working on, theoretical essays on John Donne and W. B. Yeats, were destroyed when the flat burnt out. He felt like he was exiting Dante's inferno: turning around to get a final glimpse, Dobrinja, once a suburb, now a scarred battlefield of burnt-out buildings. Driving down Snipers' Alley, his first time out of Dobrinja in so long he couldn't remember, he passed graffiti that someone had scrawled in white paint on a building beside the road leading into Grbavica, a suburb now controlled by Serbs: WELCOME TO HELL. His mother Zora was trapped in Grbavica, he hadn't seen her for eight months. Eighty years old with one kidney removed, living by herself, but there was no way into that neighbourhood now, past the entrance to Hell.

They were all alive, holding hands because survival, and somehow they had managed to stay alive all those months in Dobrinja, meant that, much as you loved the people around you, you had to think about yourself, put every last bit of energy into staying alive. And they still did not know where they were going to live once they got to the centre of town.

They found a place with relatives, and spent most of the days inside, hearing news of how many people had been killed each day. On 17 August, Mario could bear the isolation no more and ventured out to the Croatian Cultural Centre because he was starving: for information, for books, for conversation. It was a Monday, and he got to the Centre, and he was standing against a wall laughing at something, remembering that before the war he once gave a poetry reading with Radovan Karadzic, the man who is now pummelling Sarajevo, when suddenly, a 155 mm shell came out of nowhere and he was buried underneath the wall. For a second, he could hear nothing except his own voice screaming: 'I'm going to die, I'm going to die, I can't breathe.'

He was there for two hours before someone pulled him out. Shaking, bloody, he got himself home. The only thing he can think of now, every day, every night, is no longer the book that he was writing, the career that is forever on hold, or even the end of the war, if it will ever happen. The only thing he thinks of, from the time he wakes up to the moment he crawls between freezing cold sheets, is staying alive, staying alive, staying alive.

The rhythm of the words is a mantra that protects him: he says it over and over until it beats like a drum in his brain.

He was caught in a third mortar attack. By now, he is sure he is losing his mind. As he was being taken to hospital, he saw a woman's shoe in the road, empty and full of blood.

One day, a week after I met Mario in the Peace Centre, he told me this: 'You can kill a life without killing anyone. It's a psychological way of destroying civilians bit by bit by destroying normal life – food, electricity, water. It is a wish to humiliate, denigrate. You can conquer a city and take a city and do it in a civil manner, but you don't snipe at people, you don't butcher people, you don't cleanse villages. That's beyond normal warfare. There's something else behind it – the desire to humiliate.'

It was the longest speech that I heard him make, and I remembered every word of it three weeks later when I drove over the hills to meet the Bosnian Serbs, the ones responsible for the destruction of Sarajevo. One of the leaders of the government, Nikola Koljevic, had been a professor of English, a Shakespearean scholar at Sarajevo University, knew *King Lear* by heart, and had, in fact, been the mentor of Mario Susko. But all I could think of as Koljevic justified what his people were doing to the city where he had lived for twenty years was how odd it was to be so bitter, to hate a place so much. At the end of a long night with him, which continued past supper, past many references to *King Lear* and betrayal and blindness, Koljevic gave a shred of insight: 'Do you know,' he said, twisting himself in his chair and pointing a finger down in the direction of the darkened Sarajevo, 'they never made me a full professor. They ... never ... gave ... me ... the ... honour.' It was an enlightening moment, because it showed the Serb mentality, something that Richard West, the historian, wrote about in his biography of Tito:

Because they believe the whole world hates them, the Serbs often behave in a way that actually creates that hatred.

Mario was made a full professor, but now he can no longer teach. We are walking very quickly through town, climbing up the hill towards Bjelave, Klea's house. Even though he is terrified of being outside, Mario does not like me to walk alone in Sarajevo because I might take a wrong street, although I tell him I'm fine. He feels responsible for me, and meets me every day at the Centre, helps me to pull the 20 kg flak jacket over my head. If I can't make it because there is a press conference or I have a deadline, or I have to spend all day trying to find a satellite phone to file my copy, he gets offended, thinking that I can't bear his company because I am bored. 'I understand, I understand perfectly well why you don't like coming here.' He doesn't believe when I say that I want to see him, want to see the family. 'Everyone has abandoned us,' he says bitterly. This is a bad day, I can tell, even worse than others. 'Europe, the West, the world. I can understand it if you abandon us too.'

But I wouldn't, because they have now become a part of my life. We are moving through the market trying to buy cigarettes, because Mario has run out of pipe tobacco and is desperate for nicotine. 150 DM for a carton of Marlboro Red from a man standing in the corner wearing two coats, a hat, a scarf, ski gloves and boots. His nose is red and swollen with the cold. I hand Mario the money and he mutters about thieves and robbery and taking advantage of desperate people, but he buys them because he needs them.

He lights one while walking, shaking so that it takes three tries with the match. He shakes now, all the time. He can't sleep, he has low blood pressure, he says he is afraid to move. 'After that second incident,' he says. 'I am completely and utterly wrecked. At night I have visions of being torn to pieces.' Lights another cigarette. 'Things are bad physically, the hunger, the cold, not being able to wash. But it's worse spiritually. There's so much bitterness that you can't go anywhere, do anything.'

Once a day, after his morning walk to the Law School and hours of sitting staring at walls, he makes the five-minute walk to 95 Bjelave, where Klea, who was also burnt out of her flat, lives in a converted garage with her husband and baby. There are two rooms, always cold, and a wood stove that she frantically tries to keep going even though wood is 150 DM for a month's supply, and a tiny kitchen where she tries to make a meal with the humanitarian aid food. 'Cheese from rice! Wine from rice!' She tries to make a joke but instead her eyes fill with tears.

Klea looks like her mother. She is small and thin, with enormous blue eyes. Her face is tiny, like a lemon: she has lost so much weight since the war began that she can't wear her old clothes anymore, not the dress she was married in, not even the pair of jeans she was wearing when the bullet ripped through them, missing her leg. She keeps them, though, on the edge of her bed, because she thinks it is important to remember what is happening outside her door.

Klea's English, like her father's, is perfect. She was a child when she moved with the family to America when Mario taught at Nassau State College in New York. On bad days when the shelling is so loud they can barely hear each other talk, they try to remember everything about those seven years. Marija remembers an artificial Christmas tree with presents around it. Mario remembers 'freedom of movement. Going for walks. I remember being in London and spending hours walking through the parks. Now extreme limitation is eating me up. One day I had to cross from one street to the other, a seven-minute walk and I thought, within those seven minutes, someone could kill me 420 times – one bullet a minute. You really ask yourself what your life is worth if someone has that kind of control over it. It only takes a sniper a second to kill you, and that is what bothers me most of all. The internal exile.'

'Please don't say those things. Don't talk about the walks.' It is Marija, beginning to cry. Klea hugs her, wraps her thin arms around Marija's long grey sweater.

Mario is silent.

That exile, and the frustration that his work has stopped, his research, the three books that were about to be published when the war began, makes the war especially painful. He has been an academic since he was 21, now he cannot even read or write past 4 pm because it gets dark and there is no electricity, not even enough candles. 'It's like going blind. You can't read, you can't write, you can barely move. No electricity, no more batteries for a torch, and we're down to our last candle.' The candle, just a wick floating in a cup of oil, is the focal point for the family: they sit around it, staring, not talking, smoking only if someone has given them cigarettes, watching the flame as it grows fainter. When they have burned the night's quota – usually three or four hours' worth – they go to bed because there is nothing else to do and it is too cold to sit without the fire.

Sometimes, they all go to Klea's and play cards in the dark. They ration the food: I had one slice of bread this morning, so I can't have another one until five o'clock. There is only half a bag of macaroni left for two weeks; we can only have ten pieces each today. They chew slowly. When I brought a sausage that I had bought in Frankfurt airport on my way to Zagreb, they stared at it for five minutes before Klea ran to find a knife.

It is strange to think that people who have never been poor, who are multilingual, who have travelled, lived abroad, are now destitute, that nearly all of their waking hours are dominated by thoughts of food, or the unbearable cold.

Mario, who is sitting near the window, staring at nothing, suddenly speaks. 'It's strange how we measure our lives. You use a finger of oil in your lamp and when you use it up, you say goodnight, that's enough for one day. On the salary I make now, I can buy one newspaper a month, a loaf of bread, some milk. But all the standards we had before the war, the things one has like coffee and chocolate, just everyday stuff, disappear.'

Mario makes 12 DM a month as a full professor. Sometimes he gets paid. Sometimes he does not. He runs through the cost of food on the black market: a kilo of coffee, 30 DM. Cigarettes, 3.5 DM a packet for local ones exported across the front line from Serbia; 6 DM for Marlboro Red. A tin of beef: 20 DM. Powdered milk: 30 DM a kilo. A tin of cheese, a jar of baby food: 8 DM.

Food, and the ritual of collecting food, preparing it, making soup from old packets of spices, cheese from rice, wine from rice, is an obsession. Food comes in packages that arrive sporadically, collected from Caritas, the Catholic Relief Organisation, usually once a month. But for Neven Kordic, who is standing in a long, long queue at the Caritas office in front of the HVO (Croatian Army in Bosnia) near Bjelave, it has been two and a half months since his family received a package. The food was trapped on an aid convoy in Kisiljak, the Croat town outside Sarajevo. A package meant to keep a family alive for two weeks contains two kilos of rice, two litres of oil, potatoes, one kilo of meat, two kilos of sugar, one kilo of milk powder; one kilo of rice; half a kilo of margarine; half a kilo of fish; one tube of liver paste; one kilo of beans; one bar of soap; one kilo of detergent. The last two items are a joke because there is no water with which to wash.

What is saddest is to hear them talk about their last days of normality. That, like the food, becomes a ritual. It's like sitting in a dream; everything stops as each one remembers their life before. What burns in Sandra's mind is the turkey and sausages her grandmother cooked last Christmas. Marija remembers America, Christmas Day 1973; Klea remembers walking with

Zoran through the centre of Sarajevo last spring, 2 May 1992, the day before the heaviest shelling began, pushing Deni in a stroller. Someone photographed them that day and it ran in the newspaper on one of the last days it was printed. 'It was spring, it was warm, it was a wonderful night!' Her eyes are shining and she is, for once, really smiling. 'I think I had an ice cream, I was wearing a t-shirt, and we were not thinking about anything, just walking along and holding hands with the baby in his chair. My God, I can't imagine ever being that happy again! It was only eight months ago, but we were normal!'

Mario remembers his work. 'The worst thing of all,' he says, 'is the spiritual vacuum, not being able to work to my full potential.' He pauses for so long that I think he has finished, but he has not. 'This is not living, this is about survival. Just trying to get through the day.'

'I want to tell you about the queues,' says Marija. 'Because we measure our days by the queues.' She pulls the sweater around her shoulders, and begins to count on her long, slender fingers.

And so, there is a food queue, a water queue, a bread queue, a queue to buy wood for those who can afford the 150 DM a metre, and for those who can't there are the fights in the park for the last twig of wood. Those who are strong enough chop the wood down, those who aren't rush in when the wood falls and try to pick up the remnants. There are the queues to search for trash. Someone has discovered that if you roll old newspapers − or books because there are no newspapers anymore − tightly into a ball and sprinkle it with water and then let it sit, it hardens enough to burn for a few minutes. Mario says he would kill to feel warm just for five minutes.

The queues must be the coldest places in Sarajevo. It is Marija who stands in the bread queue every morning, between 6 and 7 am, with her scarf pulled tightly around her head like a babushka and her thick snow boots from the ski season the winter before. But they all collect water, taking the 25-litre plastic jugs and dragging them along on a sled. The gunners target water queues: they know exactly where they are and they know that people have to stand, quietly, patiently, but terrified, waiting for their bread, their water, their box of food from Caritas. That exposure cannot be avoided, and everywhere there are stories of the dead, the bodies that were found after a shell landed near a queue. There are plastic flowers now in Vase Misinka Street, in front of a shell hole, the place where seventeen people died in the bread queue massacre on 27 May 1992. Everyone says they were almost there that day.

'What do you think about when you're standing in the queue?' Sandra asks.

Mario says he thinks about death, especially since his friend was standing in line the week before and his wife was killed in front of him.

Mario finds it humiliating. Once, when the water truck had not arrived for days, Mario and Marija were sitting inside when it began to rain, and automatically, like robots, they raced outside with buckets and began to collect the rainwater. 'Suddenly, we looked up at each other and realised what we were doing. So desperate. And we went inside and tried to dry off and next day, the truck arrived. It's that kind of frustration, but also what strikes me is how people in Sarajevo have become like zombies. In Moscow, there are huge lines, but people are reading books or talking while they wait. Here, it is silent. And when I wait in line, what goes through my mind is this: I am like a zombie.'

There is a proper lunch that day, brought in my knapsack from Frankfurt: tinned ham, a loaf of bread and some cheese. No one speaks while we eat and everyone makes it last, even the glutinous ham that is too pink with preservatives, and the cheese that has frozen once on my windowsill at the hotel and is too chewy.

Sandra stops chewing and looks at me. 'Tell me,' she says, 'about the world. I haven't listened to the radio in so long because there are no batteries.'

I've got my shortwave and we tune into the BBC World Service and we sit until it is too dark to sit and then Mario walks me home.

★

There were two main hospitals functioning in Sarajevo during the war, Kosevo and the State Hospital, which was called the French hospital by locals. Both of them stank of antiseptic and blood. Cots were pushed into hallways because there was no space in the wards for all of the injured, the dying, the newborn. It was strange to think that even while surgeons were amputating limbs with minimal or no anaesthetic and removing shrapnel from screaming children, performing surgery without enough water to wash their hands, babies were still being born in another room.

There was no heat or water; if there was petrol from UNPRO-FOR the generator would run for a few hours and the surgeons would try to operate as quickly as they could. If there was no electricity, they would operate by candlelight, or by the light of a torch that one of the nurses held near the open wounds. The lifts did not work, nor the escalators: and because the cavernous rooms had been so long without heat, the cold seemed to permeate everything.

In Kosevo, I walk through the wards with Jasmina, a 23-year-old intern who talks of not being able to sterilise instruments, of how dangerous it is for people to wake up from anaesthetics to the freezing cold. The temperature inside the building is 5 below and dropping.

Jasmina says that the doctors are faced with horrible choices every day: which patient to take first; whether to use the tiny bit of petrol to run the generator or operate with a bit of heat; which patients get the scant medicines. Who gets a dressing; who gets the last of the antibiotics for a festering wound. Whether to amputate a leg that could probably heal, when you don't have enough antibiotics to ward off gangrene. Who gets the last blanket. And who gets a coffin when they die. There were only 5,000 coffins in the city: not enough for the dead.

'You know, as a doctor, you're trained to make people well, to heal them, but I can't keep them alive.' We pass the children's ward, where nearly every bed holds an amputee: a tiny stump, where once there was a leg or an arm, wrapped in bloody gauze.

Jasmina slumps into a chair and shifts her weight because the chair is so cold. She asks for a cigarette and shakes her head. 'I can't keep them alive.'

The head of the emergency ward at Kosevo, Professor Arif Smajic, sits in his office dressed in an overcoat, talking about chronic diseases and loss of blood, cold as a direct cause of death. I shuffle in the chair, if I sit for longer than five minutes cold permeates my jeans, Gortex jacket, thermals. He apologises for the cold in the room and says, 'We have had winters in Sarajevo where the temperatures dropped to 30 below. The only hope we have got now is our friendship with God Almighty.'

Outside the hospital, a few metres away, it is Christmas week in Sarajevo. The city, in the thick grey fog of winter seems surreal, like a film set from earlier in the century. People, unsmiling and terribly thin, move through the streets dragging sleds or pushcarts laden with water bottles or stacks of wood. The stench of wood fires, of open sewers, of rubbish tipped into the gutters, rises up even through the cold. This is what it must have been like to live a thousand years ago: without water, without sanitation, without medicine, light, heat, and in the constant presence of barbarism. When you are that frightened, that cold and that hungry, all that matters is getting food to eat and a place to sleep.

There are no Christmas specialties this year, no cakes or sausages or ham, but around the market square someone has found tinsel left over from the year before, when there was no war, and has draped it around the stalls. Thick Croatian brandy, Stock, which tastes like cough syrup, is selling for 100 DM a bottle, and one old woman has hoarded her ration supplies and is selling eggless sugarless biscuits. 'You know, Bosnians are synonymous with disorganisation,' says Spomenka Beus, a beautiful 48-year-old former university professor who lives alone with her son Ivo. 'Not only the fact that you go to the black market and try to buy a bottle of cognac for 80 DM – ten times what you would pay in a duty-free. That's annoying enough. But then you have this little voice whispering in your ear: "Lady, do you want to buy some French perfume?" Because at the beginning of the siege, someone robbed the drugstores. Which is why we can no longer buy toothpaste.' She can't go to the black market, because she works during the day and timing is essential: 'And so, I rely on relatives in Split, who send me packages with the UN. The last one arrived two months ago, and when I got it, I was the richest woman in Sarajevo. Smoked ham, toothpaste, chocolate.' She smiles wryly. 'But all I really wanted was some powdered milk.'

That week, there are rumours in town (because there are no newspapers, except a few copies of *Oslobodenje*, word of mouth always travels fast) that 70 per cent of the humanitarian aid is not getting through to the people, a figure that the UNHCR hotly deny.

'The aid is delivered by plane and truck then sent to central warehouses,' said a UN spokesman. 'Then it is in the hands of the government.' If, in fact, most of the food is going to the soldiers who are fighting to defend the city, said one unnamed source, then so be it. 'They're fighting to save the city,' he says. 'Every male in this city is in a uniform. They need food to stay alive.'

But the food is going to the black market as well as to the front lines. Later that week exploring Zetra, the former hockey stadium used for the 1984 Olympics, 300 metres from the Delegates' Club where General Morillon, the French UNPROFOR commander, is drinking champagne, eating food cooked by his own chef imported from Switzerland, and sitting in sandbagged rooms awash with electricity and heating, I find refugee families huddled into the underground changing rooms where athletes used to lace up their skates. It is so dank and cold that it is unthinkable that children have been living here, playing on the floors, without sunlight, for six months. Amra Kurbegovic, who has two children with her, says she moved into Zetra when her house was destroyed by a shell. 'I ate an apple last week that came in a package from the Seventh Day Adventists,' she says. 'When I bit into the apple, my jaw ached from chewing it. I had not chewed food for that long.'

The other half of Zetra is used to store food and, after sitting with families who live on rice and macaroni, it is like walking into a fantasy. Miles and miles of food, sent from England, France, Italy: boxes of Smash, McVitie's biscuits, clothes from Feed the Children, boxes of vitamins, lentils, rice, dried vegetables, all just sitting in a warehouse. I feel sick at the sight of it, thinking of the Suskos and the sausage from Frankfurt: the one that took thirty minutes to eat.

'Just tell me, what is it for?' I ask a UN official later that day. 'Please tell me, I'm naïve, I'm stupid, but people are starving and you've got all that food? Explain it to me, please.'

He looks bored. He explains, again, that once it gets to the warehouses, it is in the hands of the Bosnian government. Perhaps they are stockpiling it for a disaster.

Isn't this already a disaster?

No, he says. It is going to get worse.

★

A week before Christmas, the cold got worse, and so did the shelling: in four days, nearly 500 people tried to get out of the city at night by crossing the airport runway which separated two front lines. They were caught by the UN, who estimated that around 130 people tried to cross each night – some soldiers, but mainly refugees, or black marketeers carrying food. They were sent back. 'We believe that with winter coming quickly, people are probably better off trying to stay in the city than climbing over those mountains,' a UN spokesman said. And yet, day after day, people would try to get out of the city. They had no idea where they would go once they had crossed the mountain path into Central Bosnia; how they would get to Croatia, and if, in fact, they would be allowed in once they had reached the border. All they wanted was to get out.

In the intensive care ward at Kosevo hospital, Peter Kessler from the UNHCR told us that the mortality rate was one person dying from the cold every two days. 'Of 114 people, 35 have died in the past few months,' he said. 'This is an example of what we are going to see. People are dying from the cold.'

A few days before Christmas, I walk to Bjelave and find Klea huddled inside. Deni is sick with a cold and she says she has stopped going out to collect water because her neighbour was ten metres from an exploding shell in the water queue. But she is singing that morning, because she has saved enough flour to make pita bread to eat with cheese, given to her by a Muslim neighbour. She has saved two potatoes for twenty days to stuff the pita with, and she is going to make *buhtl*, a kind of doughnut.

'Last Christmas, we had stockings, red with white trim. Left in Dobrinja, probably burnt.' Her face darkens. 'I got gold earrings, Deni got toys. This year, nothing.'

She believes she was lucky to find the house where they are living, even though it is 35 metres from the front line. 'It's strange how dead my things look now ... the television set, the radio. What I miss now are my records. Things like Dire Straits or Bruce Hornsby, or even watching the European Cup. When I finally got evacuated from Dobrinja, I don't know, I must have been crazy, but the first thing I did was ask someone who won the European soccer championship ... '

In a corner Mario is smoking his pipe, without tobacco. He says he heard that Willy Brandt died, through a colleague, one month after it happened. He says that he feels like his vision of the world has been cut so small it is now microscopic. He has no idea what is happening in Russia, in England, he asks me to explain what has happened to Mad Cow Disease, because he used to follow it. He says he used to correspond with J. G. Ballard because he had translated *Empire of the Sun* into Serbo-Croat.

There's been no mail since March 1992. Nearly one year. A battery to play the radio costs 15 DM. Mario calls it an information blockade. He stares at the silent radio, the television that has not been turned on for eight months.

'It's strange how dead these things look now,' he says.

A few days before Christmas, I wait for Mario on a corner near the old cathedral, waiting for a concert inside to begin. As I walk to meet him from the Holiday Inn, there are people chopping wood near the Miljacka River, hacking away at the ruins of furniture. There are Serb snipers positioned directly across the river, but when I stop to talk to an older woman who is bent under the weight of the wood strapped to her back, she laughs.

'If the sniper doesn't get us,' she says. 'The cold will.'

The walk – or the run because at every intersection that faces the river I hold my breath and run as fast as I can across it – takes about twenty minutes. Along the way, I walk through the old town, past the Sarajevska Pivara, the beer factory, which oddly enough occasionally has heat and where I sometimes go when I can bear it no longer and sit on top of a radiator. In front of it is a water tap and behind that is a long queue. The people stand, diving behind walls when the sniper across the river shoots at them.

One man is reading a book. He is in fairly good spirits because when he woke this morning and threw open his window, he saw the fresh snow. For one moment, he forgot where he was and how he was living. At first he thought that maybe he would go skiing; that's what he would have thought in the old days. Then there was the hollow sound of shooting, and he remembered. He suddenly had the brilliant idea of using the water to wash. He is faintly sardonic now. 'My life is now worth one litre of water and one kilo of bread,' he says, introducing himself with a slight bow. Mirza Sivalija, 61 years old, a Muslim. 'And for dessert, there is one kilowatt of electricity. No one will ever forget this winter.'

Inside, the church is full; people are standing in the aisles, blocking the doorways, sitting on each other's laps, standing shoulder to shoulder. There is no holy water, no incense, no heating. Some of the women are wearing their fur coats left over from another lifetime, and the last bits of their lipstick, with the last silk scarves that they managed to save wrapped around their necks. The man next to me is shivering with cold, but when the music begins, he stops. On the altar, a woman with a fur coat and red lipstick begins to sing. Her breath comes out like ice and she is wearing gloves. The musicians are wearing overcoats. Mario whispers in my ear: 'They are mixed, Serbs, Croats,

Muslims. But even so, if the Serbs know we're here, they'll shell us.' The concert was arranged in secret, the time circulated by word of mouth.

I go to mass on Christmas Eve at St Michael's, a shrapnel-gouged church on Snipers' Alley where the clock has stopped at one, the time of the first shelling. It's midnight and the Reuter's correspondent and I race up to the balcony and listen: 'Silent Night' in Serbo-Croat. Communion takes twenty minutes, the line is so long, and most of them soldiers. When we leave the church, some of the soldiers begin shooting in the air and immediately the Serbs on the hill shoot back. We leave, climb the icy stairs of the Holiday Inn. Before I go to bed, I draw back my blackout curtains and stare at the darkened city; no lights, no candles, complete and utter darkness. Only the sound of the guns.

On Christmas Day, three 82 mm shells land two metres from the main entrance of the Delegates' Club, General Philippe Morillon's residence. He says, 'It's a very elegant way to wish us Merry Christmas,' but at the briefing that morning, although the attack was clearly targeted, it is not yet clear whether it came from the Bosnian or the Serb side. 'The presence of UNPROFOR in the heart of the city disturbs somebody,' Morillon says. 'I am not concerned about my life but about the lives of my soldiers.' Snow is falling lightly, and I spend two hours on the satellite phone in the Reuters office dictating my copy.

Two days after Christmas, the first heavy snow begins, and from my window on the second floor of the Holiday Inn facing the Unis Towers, I watch people pulling sleds carrying their water containers, their faces and bodies wrapped in layers of dark clothing. The snow has muffled the sound of the fighting, but it is temporary. Two weeks earlier, on 8 December, the Serbs began moving their first tanks onto the airport road, slicing the city in half, cutting it off from the outside world and making the journey down Snipers' Alley deadly even for journalists. On the hills outside the city, Zuc and Trebevic, and in Otes, soldiers are squatting in trenches covered in snow, defending the lines of the already severed city.

UNHCR now states that two people are dying from the cold every 24 hours: 'This is the beginning of what could be hundreds, perhaps thousands of people dying.' There is no wood for coffins to bury the dead; one truck that was coming from Zenica in Central Bosnia with enough planks to build 500 coffins was delayed at a checkpoint in Kisiljak. A UNICEF doctor, comparing Sarajevo to the siege of Leningrad, says that most people are existing on 700 calories a day; to stay warm enough to keep well, they need at least 1800.

In the western suburbs, the Serbs are pushing to sever the city. I speak to one of the fighters in the suburb of Otes, an eighteen-year-old called Edin Hamzic, half-Serb, half-Muslim. Six months ago, he ran away to join the army and first fought in an anti-tank division in Dobrinja. Then he got to Otes, where he sat with his group trying to fend off tanks 40 metres away, too close to shoot. 'I always thought I was immortal,' he says, 'but during those days in Otes, I thought I would die like an animal, down in a trench, without food or air. And I realised then that while I was sitting in the trenches, working for the special forces, there were guys sitting in the headquarters in downtown Sarajevo, who didn't have a clue. Our commander, for instance, ran away to Germany six hours before Otes fell. When it did fall, I realised that we – the fighters – were doing one thing and the political leaders were doing another. And I thought, I'm not a dreamer, this is no reason to die.'

Six months later, I would see him again, in the television centre in Sarajevo where he is working for Reuters TV. By then he is recovering from a wound which has left him with a five-inch scar and a limp, and planning to go to London, bitter about the months spent in a trench, and about how close he had come to dying for an ideal he no longer believes in.

'Some people believe Bosnians can live together,' he says. 'But not with 280,000 people dead. It can never be like it was. My only regret,' he says slowly, running his hands through his cropped hair, 'is that I lost my two best friends in this war, fighting. The only good thing is that they died last summer when we all still believed in something, when we thought it was all worth it. They died believing.'

★

In Sarajevo, there were always two stories. One was what was happening on the ground, inside the city, the feelings and emotions, the living and the dead. You could take the pulse of the city by walking down the street, going to the market, the churches, the cafés. But the other story was running parallel, in New York, London and Geneva, and it changed and moved so quickly and yet so awkwardly that it was difficult, and infuriating, to follow. And inside Sarajevo, aside from the World Service on the BBC, we did not have television, newspapers or reports, and news from the outside came word of mouth: from the Reuters correspondent, from the BBC office, or from the television centre. The information came from sources, from civilians, from soldiers.

And so, on New Year's Eve day I stood outside in the parking lot of the PTT, playing with one of the children who would race up to the journalists' cars looking for bon-bons.

'*Nema bon-bon.*'

'*Imma!*' Give me!

Give me cigarette, give me bon-bon, give me give me . . .

I am waiting for a press briefing with Boutros Boutros-Ghali, Secretary General of the United Nations, who arrives surrounded by diplomatic correspondents who have trailed him for the day, and will quickly follow him out of Sarajevo. There are other people waiting for Mr Boutros-Ghali besides the press: a group of demonstrators stand in the cold, wrapped in shawls with placards: 'Please stop defending us your way. We are getting exterminated.'

We crowd a room, standing, blinking in the glare of television cameras, and wait. Boutros-Ghali looks uncomfortable and shifts slightly when a young reporter from Sarajevo raises her hand. 'Mr Ghali,' she says in a high clear voice. 'I work for Studio 99 radio station in Sarajevo. Perhaps you have heard of us? No? Well, then I would like to ask you a question. You are guilty for every single dead man, woman and child. I want to know, do you have a conscience? How many dead would be enough for you, Mr Ghali?' She sits down, shaking slightly.

Boutros-Ghali clears his throat and begins to speak. 'Our role is to find a peaceful solution ... we must engage in dialogue with all the warring parties ... ' He then goes on, to the astonishment of the reporters, to say, 'You are in a situation where there are fourteen other places in the world worse off than this.' The lack of compassion in his statement is extraordinary. At that point, some reporters walk out in fury and Tony Birtley, the ABC journalist who would later distinguish himself for his work in Srebrenica, raises his hand. 'Mr Secretary General,' he says, 'surely that must be cold comfort for the people of Sarajevo who have suffered since this war began.'

Interruption. Some of the defence correspondents ask defence questions, mainly related to the issue of UN troops on the ground, but there is little mention of the food situation, the shelling, the relentless attacks on civilians. We get up to leave and Boutros-Ghali politely wishes everyone a happy holiday. He leaves Sarajevo that afternoon.

About two weeks later, the West gives the Bosnians another

gift: the Vance-Owen Plan, a jumble of diplomacy proposing to divide Bosnia-Hercegovina into ten autonomous provinces, bound together under a weak central government. The provinces would be ethnically based, Serb, Croat and Muslim, but could not have any international legal personality, meaning they could not enter into agreements with foreign states. The country would be defined as a 'decentralised state' made up of 'constituent people' with 'most government functions carried out by the provinces'. There would be full freedom of movement with internationally-controlled highways connecting the republics. It would be demilitarised under UN/EC supervision.

On paper, the plan seems like a viable solution, something that perhaps could lead to peace. But in reality, it means that the Serbs would be rewarded with half the Bosnian territory, even though they only constitute 34 per cent of the population. The Croats, with 17 per cent of the population, would get 27 per cent. And the Muslims, who have sustained the greatest losses, and have the largest community, 44 per cent of the population, would be given 24 per cent.

The plan, after much diplomatic squabbling, rejection and revision, is eventually discarded, lost among the many attempts to carve up Bosnia. But what the plan would succeed in achieving would be the pre-empting of a more brutal war that was already beginning in Central Bosnia and on some of the front lines in Sarajevo: a war between former allies, the Croats and the Muslims. Shortly afterwards, what had been the beginning of hatred and suspicion between Muslims and Croats spirals into violence, killing and genocide, not in London, not in Geneva, where the decisions are being made, or in New York, where Boutros-Ghali is comfortable and warm, but on the ground in Bosnia.

I woke on Serbian New Year to the sound of heavy fighting and a delicate mist outside my window. In the half light, through the broken glass I could see tracer rounds from anti-aircraft guns flying between the two buildings next to the Holiday Inn. I watched the battle for twenty minutes, remembering a soldier in Central Bosnia who said he never knew how to fire a gun before the war but was very good at video games. Sometimes, the sounds of the machine guns rang, almost in harmony, and some of the waiters at the hotel said the soldiers were sending each other messages, football songs. They had gone to school together before, now they were only separated by trenches.

I was going home soon. My rotation in Bosnia was almost over and I was planning to leave: to stuff my backpack with the sleeping bag, the hiking boots, the wool socks, the Gortex that never seemed warm enough. And to leave behind everything else, thinking that I would get back and try to forget everything, to begin other stories, to celebrate Christmas. But everything about Bosnia made it impossible to forget. On 13 January another peace plan in Geneva failed, the same day a British soldier, Wayne Edwards, from Wrexham, was shot dead by an HVO soldier near Gornij Vakuf in Central Bosnia.

I flew to Split on a Monday. When the Hercules took off, I looked down at the city, covered in snow, the mountains split by rivers and I was flooded with emotions – relief, guilt, hunger, claustrophobia. I was thinking about Mario and Marija and about how easy it was to walk into their lives and then walk out. I was going to get a shower, going to eat fish and use the telephone. I was going to wake up in a bed with blankets, not covered with my sleeping bag, and not sleeping in every piece of clothing I own. Wake up to the sound of the radio, not a mortar thud and the hotel shaking. Walk out a door and not run, not wonder who was watching me and whether or not my jacket was attracting too much attention.

The day before I left, I walked to Bjelave and took some

letters from Klea to post in England, and a shopping list of things to bring to Sarajevo when I came back in February: five packets of Amphora pipe tobacco some jars of baby food, preferably vegetables, fuses, batteries for the radio.

And a message for the American Embassy in Zagreb, some information about getting out of Sarajevo as US citizens.

I was shifting my feet; I hate saying goodbye. I was feeling terribly guilty. 'Is that all? No chocolate, no whisky?'

Mario saw the discomfort on my face. He laughed, that terrible laugh that is not really funny, more sardonic, more mad.

'That's all. Go, leave now, go to England, forget this. There is nothing left here but the dead.'

'Are you coming back?' Marija called from the chair where she sat holding Deni. He was screaming, his ear was infected.

'Yes,' I said.

'Then don't wait too long, and be careful.'

But I never saw them in Sarajevo again. One month later, Marija, Mario and Sandra flew to Zagreb on a UN relief flight and then to London. I met them at the airport in a taxi, a Mercedes, to take them to the train station. Mario had a job, nine months at the University of East Anglia. Sandra was miserable; she did not want to leave Sarajevo, Klea, Deni or Zoran, whose papers I was still trying to arrange. She climbed the stairs to a café in Heathrow, ordered a cup of tea and burst into tears. 'Darling,' her mother said, stroking her hair.

'You should be happy,' her father said. She stared at him.

Later, we drove around Buckingham Palace and Marija began to cry. 'I never wanted to be a refugee,' she said, running her hands over the front of her coat.

'We don't mean to sound unappreciative,' Mario said, 'but all we really want is our old life back.'

'Not now,' Sandra said. 'We will have it but not now.' It was misty in London, not as cold as Sarajevo, but grey. It must have been strange for them to see people on the streets, not running, walking slowly with bags and eating food on the pavement. They seemed tired and shocked, worn out.

I had planned a lunch, but Mario and Marija weren't hungry and Sandra wanted a hamburger from MacDonald's. We drove on through London in silence, their three small bags in the back of the car all that was left of the old life and the only sound was of Marija rubbing her hands, completely chapped from the wood she had chopped in Sarajevo.

THE QUICK

AUTUMN 1992-AUTUMN 1993

THE FIRST TIME I MET Gordana Knezevic, the deputy editor of *Oslobodenje*, the Sarajevo daily newspaper, was in the early winter of 1993. She said this: 'We are only alive, you and me and everyone in this room, because of one thing and one thing only.' She paused and lit a cigarette, her fifth in the half hour that I had been with her. Something terrible had happened five minutes before. We had been sitting in the room, contemplating the latest ceasefire, wondering how long it would last, when a shell fell very close, and a Bosnian reporter came running into the room where we sat, white-faced, tense, clutching some paper, shouting that he had just seen a dog running away from the place where the shell landed with a human hand in its mouth. Gordana's mouth twisted and she played with her long hair. 'We are only alive through coincidence. Only because someone on that hill may or may not see you and has decided not to pull the trigger. Remember that.'

Why did some live and others die? Was it chance, or caution – crossing the street at the right time, with just enough agility and speed to avoid the snipers, staying in a basement for the duration of the bombardment? By deftly avoiding the market, the hospital, the Presidency building, the stretch of land near the river easily reached by the gunners in the Jewish cemetery? If you avoided the areas most frequently targeted, as Mario Susko did, if you stayed off the streets and only went out once a day at the same

48

time to the same location to get the same amount of water, could you manage to keep yourself alive?

There are numerous explanations that the living have, numerous superstitions and stories, and they tell the stories of the dead like parables. You see, even if you protect yourself, this might happen. If you wear a flak jacket, you stand a better chance, but only if the sniper is shooting at the middle part of your body, not your head or your neck. Then there are the exceptions that defy rules, the stories that prove all the superstitions, all the precautions wrong. A BBC reporter, always wore a light suit for superstitious reasons, but one day, doing a standup, he got hit. A *Daily Telegraph* reporter stepped out of an armoured car in which he was travelling with the British Army near Vitez, and within five minutes a Croat soldier detonated a land mine near him and he was thrown to the ground. But they both lived.

Stranger stories. During a mortar attack, a young woman threw herself on top of her baby daughter to protect her: the baby died; the mother, frantically trying to breathe live into her daughter, lived.

A Bosnian soldier on the front line stood for four hours at a time in an anti-sniper position in an abandoned building in Dobrinja. He and his best friend took turns at the gun, but never separated, never left the room without each other. One day, he broke his superstitious rule and decided to have a cigarette in the bombed-out hallway. The minute he lit up, a rifle grenade blew through the position and took off his friend's head. One lives, one dies.

A reporter for *Oslobodenje* constantly worked the streets, chasing mortars, driving down Snipers' Alley in an unarmoured Volkswagen with the windows blown out and covered up with black paper. He survived the worst part of the war without a scratch, but his wife, who spent all of her time indoors because she was too frightened to go outside, was shot through the head by a sniper one day as she stood near the kitchen window. It was the first day of yet another ceasefire. She was killed instantly.

A fourteen-year-old soldier was standing near a wall while in the next room his mother hunched over a pot of water, scrubbing his uniform. A mortar tore through the wall and he was protected from the shrapnel by that wall; his mother caught a piece in her throat and died in front of him five minutes later.

And so on and so on. The question that remained unanswered as the months of siege progressed was, who lived and who died? And at what point did you accept your fate and stop fighting the inevitable?

★

Jolanda Tabak believes that she has stayed alive because she has, in a sense, outwitted death. There was only one time when she really thought she would die, and that was during the battle of Stup when she was fighting on the front line. Most of her male colleagues died around her as the Serbs closed in on their position and she was trapped underground for hours. After something like that happens to you, nothing is ever so terrible.

Since the war began, Jolanda has lived three lives. First, in the earliest days of the war, she was a banker, then a front-line fighter, now she is a policewoman. She is alive, she would say, because she wanted to be, even though for nearly two years she was surrounded by guns and trenches and dying soldiers.

I have a very clear mental image of her. She's tall, lanky, early thirties, with long dark hair, and she's standing in the middle of a parking lot off Snipers' Alley in Sarajevo, dressed in a tight grey wool uniform, carrying her gun. It's a Kalashnikov, and she holds it the way some mothers hold their children. There's broken glass everywhere from windows that have been blown out by mortars, and pieces of asphalt ripped out of the ground where shells landed. There's a crowd of children, wild after two years of war, screaming in the distance, and the sound of United Nations trucks rolling by. It's October 1993, hazy autumn weather and for the first time since the war began, it's quiet – no shooting from the hills, no whistle of grenades. But for anyone who has lived in Sarajevo throughout the war, it's a terrible, unpredictable quiet, and Jolanda is looking over her shoulder towards the hills on the other side of the road where the Serb snipers used to shoot from. It's a natural reflex: everyone in Sarajevo does it.

Jolanda's on duty, getting ready for the night shift, 8 pm to 8 am. She's wearing full makeup, which she has carefully applied even though she doesn't have electricity, with hair neatly brushed, but dirty, because carrying water up the four dark flights of stairs to the one room where she lives with her mother and brother takes too much effort. Shampoo, even soap, is hard to find, but Jolanda still hoards her candy-pink lipstick and her iridescent eyeliner. Before the war, when she and her friends talked about the possibility of Sarajevo being drawn into a conflict that had already engulfed Slovenia and Croatia, she did not stock up on cans of food or candles or batteries. She bought makeup: jars of powder, pots of eyeshadow, tubes and tubes of mascara, packets of hair dye. It seemed like a small form of resistance. One way of controlling a life which had begun to spiral wildly out of control. Every day, she sits down in the dank room and continues the ritual: the cream stroked on the cheeks, the eyeshadow brushed over the brow, the carefully outlined lipstick. Even when she comes home from work, exhausted, her makeup is still intact.

She performs her ritual because it was something she did before – before the war. Now, those days seem like a dream to her. She worked in a bank downtown as a financial consultant, a yuppie job, and life meant working, coming home for a nap and then going out with her boyfriend of eight years, Fuad. There were cafés, discos, parties, cinema, theatre, Italian clothes, perfume from France. Summer at the beach, winter trips to Venice, magazines, books, friends. 'Sarajevo was the most beautiful town,' she says tonelessly. Restaurants were packed with people eating plates of meat, and the memory of that food, of even coffee with sugar, is painful.

Those days, early 1992, she was aware of a war going on in another part of Yugoslavia, and of the upcoming Bosnian referendum, but she existed in a kind of bubble of security. War was remote, far away. She, like everyone she knew, was thoroughly mixed – Slovenian mother, Croat father, Muslim boyfriend. How could there possibly be a war in Sarajevo? And besides, she reasoned, neighbours did not wake up after living together for years and begin hating each other, slaughtering each other. Sarajevo was too liberal, intellectual, civilised. Jolanda remembers thinking, sometime during that last pre-war winter of 1992: it could not possibly happen here.

It did happen. We're sitting in the crowded room she shares with her mother and her brother, but she's moving back in time, trying to focus on everything, every detail of what happened to her and on how a life can completely splinter.

December 1991 – the European Community recognised Slovenia and Croatia. This followed the Serb war of aggression against both former Yugoslavian states. The Slovenian war lasted ten days in the summer of 1991, because the military was prepared and well-armed. The Croats, who fought for nearly eight months, sustained massive losses: nearly 25,000 people were killed or missing; one-quarter of Croatian territory was seized by the Serbs. Dubrovnik was surrounded and shelled, Vukovar was levelled. Thousands of people, trying to defend their farms and villages, were slaughtered, tortured, detained, and the Croatian government signed a ceasefire in January 1992.

The Serbs then moved on to Bosnia. Their first objective was to conquer and destroy Sarajevo, a city that symbolised everything they despised: racial tolerance, multi-ethnicity, a cosmopolitan sophistication that the Serbs – who were deeply conscious of the fact that Bosnians referred to them as 'hill people' *papak* – wanted to destroy.

The intention of Slobodan Milosevic, the president of Serbia, and Radovan Karadzic, president of the so-called *Republika Srpska*, was clear. They did not attack Sarajevo just to perform genocide, to eliminate the people (nearly 30 per cent of whom were Serbs), but to level the past, to forget, to wipe out history which, they felt, had greatly aggrieved them. Their plan was to destroy the monuments, the buildings, the bridges, the city and then to eliminate the people.

Start at the beginning. There are various versions of the exact day, but to most people in Sarajevo, the third war launched by Serbia in the former Yugoslavia began on 6 April 1992 when the United States and the European Community gave diplomatic recognition to Bosnia-Hercegovina. That was also the day of the first shells and all week there was a strange feeling in Sarajevo, an acute tension in the air as though a string held taut would soon snap.

6 April. The first mortar shells fell on Sarajevo that afternoon. But in the early morning, before the protest marches and the shooting and the house-to-house fighting between city police units and Serbian gunmen, Jolanda woke up, made thick Turkish coffee and turned on the television.

There were barricades on the streets. Later in the afternoon a protest was organised, meant to be a peaceful protest, the last attempt to stop the fighting which then seemed inevitable. The first Serbian snipers took up positions on the roof of the Holiday inn and began shooting into the crowd.

The city had mobilised. As soon as the first Bosnian barricades went up in support of the government – erected by the Patriotic League, the fledgling Bosnian Army, founded at the beginning of 1991 – there was a sense of the unstoppable. Militias were formed. Overnight, war had broken out. Jolanda stayed home all day with the doors locked and the windows closed, glued to the television. She alternated between the television and the radio news: and she began to feel afraid. That night she saw Fuad. Outside, the streets were full, but people were panicked. The next day the airport was packed and Jolanda saw people running, carrying suitcases, boxes, sacks. 'See you in a few weeks, when all of this madness is over,' they called to each other, locking their apartments behind them. Nothing will happen, she told herself. This is Sarajevo. But that night, she knew that something had changed in their lives forever.

She became a front line soldier. One day she was walking to the bank, which, ludicrously, was still open even though there was no money, and something snapped inside her. It was the end of May. The Red Cross had just reported more than 1,000 bodies lying in the hospital with no space to bury them. 'I couldn't stay in the bank when everything was happening,' she says. 'I wanted to save the city.' She had never fired a gun before, not even carried one or cleaned one, but she marched into the civil police, then the core of the resistance army, and said, I want to do something. The amused soldier on duty told her that they already had a cook. She stood glued to the spot and said she wanted to fight. He looked at her and told her to come back the next day. 'On 8 June 1992,' she says proudly, 'I became a fighter.'

She learned how to shoot, how to live in a trench, how to dive from mortars, how to snipe. She was the only woman on the front line, in a battle that was taking place in her former neighbourhood. They had hardly any weapons, sometimes only pistols against Serb heavy artillery, but she used to make jokes about her lethal high-heeled boots. Those days, the beginning of the war, there were no uniforms: she wore jeans, a t-shirt and her high-heeled boots in the trenches. And nail polish and makeup, always. Once when she was on lookout duty at 2 am, she had to go check a position, but she carefully reapplied her lipstick before ducking her head and running out under fire. When another soldier asked her what she was doing, putting on makeup in the middle of a firefight, she told him calmly that you never knew when you might get lucky.

She did not think about dying. One night she convinced herself that if she did die, it was better that it was her, a single woman with no children, than a 21-year-old soldier with a wife and two kids. She was tired of seeing the innocents suffer: beautiful young girls with their legs shot off just because they happened to be crossing the wrong street at the wrong time of day. Jolanda knew, even if she was frightened, even if her boyfriend of eight years left her, that she was doing the right thing. 'There was nothing else to do.'

And then, on the worst night, during the battle of Stup, she was pinned down with heavy artillery and anti-aircraft rounds coming down like rain. For five minutes only she thought, this is it, this is where I die. Her friend Josic was killed next to her. But her fear lasted only a few minutes, because then she had to think clearly, to run, to aim, to shoot. Sometime during that night she thought of herself, two years before, sitting behind her desk at the bank, in her neat suit with her hair tied back; how could she ever have imagined she would be running in a trench, the only woman, carrying her gun. 'The war changed me. I used to be a pacifist. I don't believe in fighting and killing, I'm a sensitive . . . ' Her eyes widen. 'I'm a woman. And I don't know now if I killed anyone. Fighters never know.'

In the beginning of 1994, after nearly two years at the front, she became a policewoman. Now she works with criminals, prostitutes, gangsters instead of snipers. Her life gets increasingly bizarre.

'I never thought of myself as brave,' she says. 'Maybe crazy. My favourite colours are black and white and a psychiatrist would say I am unpredictable. Maybe. Maybe I wanted to prove myself as a woman, as a fighter. Or maybe I just wanted to help save my city.'

She also wants her life back. She says she and Fuad split up because you can't be in love and be a fighter, but she says she's a romantic, she misses simple things like trams, cars in the street, nights in Sarajevo, and the springtime. She missed the last two springs, because she was on the front line.

There was a poster in Gordana Knezevic's old office opposite the Presidency building downtown, a stark white poster with a drawing of a burnt-out building and the words: Do You Remember Sarajevo? She read it every time she sat down at her manual typewriter. She read it as she commissioned stories from writers who had not left their houses for a year, as she edited a newspaper without electricity and tried to gather information in a city under siege without access to computers, televisions or foreign newspapers.

I used to think of what Gordana Knezevic told me about coincidence all the time: when I left the Holiday Inn, when I walked to her office, when I drove with her, in an unarmoured Volkswagen with the windows blasted out and replaced with black paper, to the *Oslobodenje* building, 150 metres from Serb sniper positions. Her staff worked in an underground atomic bunker that had been built in the paranoid Tito days. The building was trashed, hit so many times by heavy artillery that it no longer resembled a structure. Three of the staff had been killed, twenty wounded and twenty members of their families killed. I remember one reporter, Marija, saying how she would leave her apartment on the eleventh floor of a tower block in Ali Pashas Polje with her best friend, Senad Gubelic, a photographer. The least dangerous route was across a muddy riverbed, they would hold hands and then slide on their stomachs into the entrance. Inside, they would race up to the third floor, out of breath, shaking, but alive.

Even so, Senad dressed up for work every day – waistcoat, leather tie, starched white shirt and shiny city shoes. 'It was important to me, from the beginning of the war, to lead a normal life. Why should I let myself go because there is a war?' Marija got married to a UPI correspondent, Kevin Sullivan, who was wounded when his armoured car drove over a mine in Central Bosnia. They now live in Singapore. But Senad kept working, sleeping most nights in a converted shower room. His bed was a plank laid across two sinks and he kept a photograph of his colleague, Salko Hondo, killed in a mortar attack, taped to the wall, next to his damaged cameras, his rolls of unused film.

'Some live, some die, some live, some die,' he would say, fiddling with a Madonna tape inside his shower room. 'You never know. Some nights I used to lie here and a mortar would come crashing down through the roof in the next room. I was okay. And sometimes you just lie here and hear the sound of the gunfights.'

Knezevic, a 44-year-old Belgrade-born Serb, has always considered herself a Bosnian. She believes that Serbs deliberately targeted the newspaper. 'Because we are what they despise – a multi-ethnic, multinational mixture of Serbs, Croats and Muslims working together. We are proof that there can be a common ground.' She says the best report to come out of the war was a story from a Serb journalist about the Muslim cemetery, and before the war, before the first artillery round set the building on fire on 10 June 1992, the word *Oslobodenje* – liberation – was spelled out in Roman and Cyrillic script. Now *Oslobodenje* is a shell on Snipers' Alley. Inside the building normal life is grotesquely parodied – a calendar burnt on 1 May 1992, a half-destroyed Serbo-Croat dictionary, silenced telexes, a map of the world, the clock stopped at noon, a poster of Natalie Wood and Warren Beatty in *Splendor in the Grass*. There is glass and rubble everywhere, but downstairs, every morning at dawn, the printing presses begin to run.

'They wanted us to have prehistoric conditions,' Knezevic says. 'They wanted to reduce us to the primitive, make us struggle to be human beings. But nothing, not guns, not tanks, not threats on our lives could silence us.' Every day, even without ink, without paper, without electricity, water, without phones, despite the fact that the building was hit 200 times, the paper came out. Within an hour, all 10,000 copies would be sold out, and then passed throughout the city. 'It became a lifeline, a symbol of normality,' she says. 'There were two semblances of normal life in the city – the bakery and the newspaper.'

There were editorials, features, foreign news that had to be sent via radio amateurs in Zagreb. But the part of *Oslobodenje* everyone turned to first was the obituaries section, two or more pages in an eight-page newspaper. People would come to the office, or to Knezevic's home, and tearfully pass on hand-written notes, or photographs. She would take them, read them and shake her head. 'For the last time, hello to our friend Zlatan Saraljic, who died on the front lines of Sarajevo for Bosnia.'

Now, two years after the war began, eight press awards later, there is a sense of 'personal victory' from never having missed a day, but Knezevic is exhausted. The absurdities of living under siege for two years, the struggle to find a candle or a cigarette, let alone keep a newspaper going, have sapped her energy. On the day of the NATO's deadline in February 1994, I climb the stairs to her apartment on Kosevo hill and find her huddled inside her dark flat wrapped in a blanket. It's a Sunday, a day she is normally at her desk downtown, but she says she didn't go in 'because I am in such a bad mood I don't want to let the others catch it'. She takes a cigarette from a pack and looks for some matches. Despite the fact that she and her husband Ivo, the Bosnian Minister of Information, are among the most influential people in Sarajevo, there is no heat, no electricity in her flat, and naturally no water. 'All energy is used for survival. In my case, survival of the family, and keeping the paper alive, having it come out every single day.'

Throughout the war, she worked constantly – eighteen-hour days, seven days a week. When she was not working, she was returning home exhausted to the flat where she lives with Ivo and her younger son, Boris. Her elder son, Igor, is in England, and her daughter, Olga, is in Zagreb. The decision to send them away at the beginning of the war is probably the thing that torments her most. She is not sure who will bear the greater psychological scars: the two who were safe, but separated from the family, or Boris, who stayed, but lived through the horror.

'On the 2nd of May, 1992, I made a quick decision to have my six-year-old daughter leave Sarajevo. My elder son was fifteen at the time. It was not planned. I was at the airport at the beginning of the war, and it was like Saigon – cargo planes packed with people trying to get out. I came home and said I didn't want my family to travel the road of refugees, but my husband and I thought, yes, we will send them. They will be back in two months.' It has now been two years, and life becomes increasingly difficult for Boris. Gordana laughs. 'He's a teenager now and he doesn't listen to me. But how can I punish him? What can I take away from him that he already doesn't have? One day I realised the only thing I could deprive him of was cutting the firewood. That was his punishment. You can't go to the basement and cut the firewood!'

One year later, another spring, it is peacetime again in Sarajevo: the trams are running, the UN says the electricity may be on in a few weeks' time. But Knezevic, who has chronicled the war from her small dark office, huddled over a manual typewriter, still does not feel the flood of relief. Not yet. She once said that what she missed most was reading the newspapers outside in the garden. She says that she could get used to peace very quickly, and yet, despite the ceasefire, she is still sceptical. 'Each moment I am testing this fear and seeing if it can be replaced with security. Not yet. During the worst shelling, we just wanted it to stop. Now it has stopped, but something is still wrong. We want justice, and we are not sure justice will come.'

There are too many bitter memories: it is only weeks since the market massacre in which 68 people died and 200 were wounded, and she still thinks of the members of staff, the friends and colleagues that she has lost.

It is February 1994. I am sitting with Gordana again in her flat and we are talking about the end of the war. The moments that stay with her are these: 'The second day of May, 1992, because it was the day my children left. Also, the day the post office burnt down, the day they tried an infantry attack on the Presidency.' She pauses and fishes for a cigarette inside her bag. 'We have a different kind of amnesia. Our forgetting is very human because if we kept all the disasters in our minds ... we would go mad. We are not really aware, and yet I believe that we are taking a place in history.'

★

Who else survived? A family of ten who lived high on a hill above Sarajevo, in a house that was only partially finished with no electricity, no heat, holes in the roof where the snow had broken through. One son, a front-line fighter. A father who lost everything. An eldest daughter who watched the younger kids like the little old lady in the shoe. A mother outside Sarajevo, trying, ironically, to get in. Children who roamed the streets with their laces untied, but who knew exactly how to avoid snipers and who could identify weapons, who knew the standard Sarajevo war phrases like 'Welcome to Hell' and 'What can we do, this is a war?'

The first time Fatima Kafedzic cried after the war broke out was when she got a letter from her eldest daughter. 'Please try to come home, if you can.' Atka, who was 22 at the time, wrote: 'We are okay, we are all alive, but my hair has turned grey.'

It was one of those bizarre twists of fate: everyone in the world was trying to get out of Sarajevo, to escape from hell, but Fatima, a 44-year-old aid worker and mother of ten, was trapped outside the city, trying to get back to her family. Her eldest son, Mehmed, was fighting somewhere on the front line, her younger children were still babies. She had been gone for seven months. It was Atka who had to run from the snipers every day to get to the water queue, Atka who was scrounging for food for all of them, and Atka who would try to explain to the littlest ones when to run and when to hide in the basement. Already, they had stopped calling her sister and started calling her Mommy.

The day the war began, Fatima – who married at nineteen after meeting her husband through a personal ad calling for a good Muslim girl – woke up in a hotel in Vienna, where she was working for CARE, preparing to bring 30 tonnes of medicine into Sarajevo. She turned on the radio. War had broken out in her city. She threw her clothes into a bag and raced to the airport. 'I'm sorry,' the polite Austrian woman at the airlines counter said. 'There are no more flights to Sarajevo. The airport has closed.' Fatima began to shout that she had to get back, at any cost. 'I'm sorry,' the woman said firmly.

She went back to the hotel and phoned her husband: it was true, there was fighting. Every day she talked to him until the phone lines to Sarajevo, her only link to them, were cut. 'That day, I panicked,' she says. 'My eldest son was fighting somewhere. The only way I could make contact with the children was through amateur radio operators and journalists who took messages and letters.' One day, a letter arrived. She found out that her husband Ahmed's two brothers had been killed, one by mortar, one by sniper, and that her nephew had lost a leg.

The next few months passed in a haze. She went south, to Zagreb in Croatia, and worked with refugees, living with them in a camp. She tried to evacuate her family, but could only get three of her teenaged daughters out on the last convoy from Sarajevo and eventually they settled in Zagreb. The other seven children were left behind in a house without electricity or water, or a bathroom even, because they had only begun building it at the start of the war. On the radio and television she saw pictures, images of Sarajevo: the maternity clinic on fire with 70 pregnant women and 173 babies inside; the bread queue massacre at the end of May in which 17 people were killed and 160 injured. To watch it, to see your city in flames, in ruins, and know your children are there and you cannot protect them was unbearable. 'Then, one day, something inside me broke,' Fatima says. 'I couldn't evacuate them, so I had to join them.' It took her one month: a bus journey to Split, a ride through southern Bosnia, and finally arriving at the last Bosnian checkpoint outside the city. The UN could not help get her in, so she walked, with a Bosnian soldier as a guide, across two front lines, and through the constant shooting. She ran, then walked, arriving in Dobrinja, one of the most dangerous suburbs. The first things she noticed were the graveyards in front of apartment buildings.

Then the buildings shot to pieces, the blockades, the burnt stump of *Oslobodenje*. As she walked, she saw shops destroyed, looted, burnt. 'I was entering this city, my home, and I had no idea how many people I knew had been killed.' In Lions Cemetery, which had been a park when she left, a place where she had taken the babies to play, there were more than 2,000 graves of soldiers and civilians. Fresh mounds of dirt with wooden crosses or crescents on top of them, and mourners lying flat above them because the snipers on the hills were constantly picking people off as they wept by the graves.

When she got to her house in Gorica, on the hill overlooking the city, she stopped outside the door. The little ones rushed to hug her: then they were telling her where to stand, where not to stand, where to run, so that she wouldn't get shot. She couldn't believe how much they had changed: both physically and mentally. 'It made me so sad when the children were telling me the difference between the sound of guns and artillery, the difference between the sound of the general alert, and the air-strike alarm. But I was proud of them. No matter how sorry I felt, I was proud that they had survived in the worst of conditions.'

She went to work. She didn't stop working, because it was one way of not thinking about the destruction around her. First there were the children: seven of them at home, needing to be fed; there was her 77-year-old mother; there was her husband. The basics of living meant finding water, getting packages of humanitarian aid (beans, rice and pasta, never enough for all of them) and telling them gently that no, they could not have bananas or chicken or meat. She did not think about what she describes as 'the good life' before the war: the days when her husband's textbook publishing business pulled in a steady profit, when the family spent three months a year travelling, when they stayed in hotels and sat on terraces overlooking the sea.

She had begun as a charity worker in the early days of the Slovenian war, in the spring of 1991, getting mothers to sign petitions against the draft, organising a resistance group called Fortress of Love. On 25 April, some of them drove to the JNA (former Yugoslavian Army) headquarters in Belgrade and stood outside until a general would see them. The secretaries came out and told this group of women, these middle-class Sarajevo housewives, that no one could see them, but that their sons would soon be home, there would never be a war.

When the war broke out in Croatia a few months later, Fatima was convinced 'that the worst things in the world were going to happen to Bosnia. It was only a matter of time.' In August, she and 5,000 other mothers from Sarajevo boarded buses and again travelled to Belgrade. This time, there were no smiling secretaries: instead, they were kept under guard for twenty-seven hours, threatened, abused. 'No, we weren't frightened,' she says defiantly. 'We were fighting for our children.' She kept travelling, lecturing, speaking.

Her greatest challenge was to keep the family together, but terrible things came out of the war. Her family was split apart, some of them were killed. 'But wonderful things also happened,' she says, dreamily. In the spring of 1993, Atka met and fell in love with the war photographer Andrew Reid. Sometime in the summer, they left the city together.

I was with Atka, who had looked after her nine brothers and sisters alone for seven months during the worst fighting in the city, soon after she left Sarajevo. We were in a marketplace in a Croatian seaside town, staring at a stack of oranges and lemons. 'I wish I could take all of that back for Sarajevo,' she said in a small voice. But she knew she could not. Shortly afterwards, she and Andrew left for New Zealand where they now have a baby son. The day of the market massacre, she was watching CNN and saw her brother Mehmed on the television screen, loading dead bodies into a truck. She panicked; even when a fax reached her in New Zealand to say everyone was safe, she did not believe them, because that is the legacy of Sarajevo. Even when you leave, you are still afraid.

Miles and miles away from Atka, on a hill overlooking Sarajevo, Fatima is still rising at first light and carrying water to the children, slicing the bread, chopping the wood, and brushing snow off the flat roof so it doesn't fall inside the holes that the mortars have made. 'It is not so bad,' she says, pausing outside where her children are playing, and despite everything, laughing. 'We are still alive.'

She's got a best friend, a Serb called Mirjana, who lives in the house below them. It's a beautiful house that Mirjana manages somehow to keep clean. She and Fatima sit together on her balcony, and from there they can look out over most of the city as they drink coffee with sugar, which Mirjana miraculously has. They talk about food. 'In the beginning of the war,' Mirjana says, 'I was saved by a bucket of fat. I spread it on bread every day, and for two weeks, we only had 50 grams of feta cheese. I don't know how we managed, but there we were.'

Mirjana is a big woman, affectionate, she grips you in a tight hug and runs her hands through your hair. It has not been easy to be a Serb in Sarajevo. She stayed because she had been married in Sarajevo, her son was born in Sarajevo, she was from Sarajevo. It never occurred to her to leave. 'I used to walk along this terrace in my bikini!' she shouts, suddenly rising up from her chair, to the city below her. 'No one is going to make me go away!'

*

If there was danger, how did you avoid it? I think that journalists often exaggerated the danger, especially when they were sitting inside the Holiday Inn or riding around in an armoured car, but there were moments, everyone had them, when you found yourself in the same equation as the Bosnians. When that happened, if you were pinned down in Lions Cemetery by a sniper for what seemed like hours, or were stuck behind a wall in Novi Travnik, or were getting shelled in your soft-skin car, you might even forget the danger in the kind of excitement that takes over when you think you've got a story that no one else has. Sometimes you got lazy and took the shortcut across a sniper's path, thinking you would be lucky. Sometimes you just forgot the danger because the city had been quiet for a few hours.

In one sense, we were equal – journalists, Bosnians – with as much chance of getting hit or losing an arm or a leg. The fact that you had a flak jacket and a helmet helped, but a flak jacket didn't cover your neck, where a sniper usually aimed. When you went out on patrol with Bosnian soldiers, you often had a false sense of security, because they would assure you that everything was alright. Of course it was alright for them, they were fighting for their country. We were just journalists sent in to report the war. Ed Vulliamy of the *Guardian* and I once spent an hour pinned down behind a wall in Novi Travnik during the start of the Muslim-Croat fighting. We had been led there by a laid-back soldier who got us back out by opening up on the sniper and giving us enough time to run to our jeep, reverse and return to Travnik as fast as the Lada could go. In *Seasons in Hell*, Vulliamy described a journey into the trenches of Bosanska Krupa with a soldier:

Is this going to be safe? '*Nema problema*,' replies Fardu. 'No problem' is the answer to everything in lackadaisical Bosnia ... He suddenly pulls us over against a house: 'This is where we have to run.'

'I thought you said *nema problema.*'

'There isn't a problem, they usually miss,' is meant to be an assurance. This time, they held their fire or didn't see us.'

Before I went to Bosnia for the first time, I read a pamphlet published by the Institute for War and Peace called *A Balkan Survival Guide for Sensible Journalists: Compiled by local hacks to prevent loss of life.* The first time I saw it, I thought it was a joke but it was not.

> ... these (Balkan) wars are not conventional conflicts. Many characteristics of Low Intensity Conflict are present – general lawlessness, a total absence of established standards of behaviour resulting in utter unpredictability, regular excesses of violence, mindless and arbitrary killings, and extremely heated chauvinistic passions bordering on the insane.

This was followed by ten points, general rules of conduct which ranged from having the best road maps available to marking your car with the word PRESS, which everyone knew really meant nothing, especially in the later days when in places like Mostar, the Croats wanted nothing better than to hit a journalist. There was information about paramilitary formations and irregulars ('avoid contact with them wherever possible as they tend to be extremists or just criminals') and a section entitled 'Whilst Under Fire':

> If fired at whilst driving, leave the car windows open as you can hear better. If the firing is coming ahead of you or from the sides, then it is generally better to make a U-turn or drive backwards as fast as you can, not forgetting to pray. Old Sarajevo hands have what they call an 'experiment in applied theology'. Sitting in the car before setting off, you ask, 'Is there a God?' and if you arrive safely at your destination you say to yourself 'There is a God!' If you are too close to the

firing positions, get the hell out and crawl for cover. If firing comes from behind then your only option is to hit the pedal. In suspect locations look for wires, strange objects and freshly dug earth, and don't stray from worn paths.

What kept the living alive was something more than being quick or driving with the windows open. It could only have been luck. Tim O'Brien, who wrote about Vietnam, recalls that in his platoon soldiers carried talismans, things like letters, P-38 can openers, their girlfriends' stockings wrapped around their necks, photographs, morphine, plasma, dogtags. In Bosnia, I noticed that most reporters had the same gear in their packs: a flashlight, a Swiss Army knife, some painkillers or morphine if you could get it, a minute Sony shortwave radio with buttons rather than a dial. But they usually had something special that they did not like to be separated from, something superstitious. The photographer Gary Knight, who walked to Gorazde in the freezing winter of 1993, had a French Army scarf that he wound around his neck; I had a lucky torch.

That torch was lucky because I had carried it with me through-out my first trip to Bosnia, when I drove into Central Bosnia to cover the fall of Jajce and the flood of refugees who carried their life possessions down the road afterwards. A photographer had given it to me: he had found it the summer before on the tenth floor of the Holiday Inn, the famous sniper floor where the Armija – the Bosnian Army – had positioned their snipers after the Serbs had been driven out of the hotel. Sometime in the summer of 1993, I passed the torch to Dr Vesna Cegnic, an anaesthesiologist at the State Hospital in Sarajevo. Her eyes were getting strained from operating by candlelight and the generators were unreliable. One day she put it down and when she turned around, it was gone. Torches with batteries were a rare com-modity in Sarajevo. Whoever got it, she said, would at least be protected. That torch had been with me in Maglaj, a city on the northern edge of Central Bosnia, forgotten by the world, but not by the Serbs. They wanted it desperately, because of its strategic position in the corridor that they wanted to carve through Bosnia, the passage that would enable them to take the first steps towards a Greater Serbia. They would be able to move freely through it from Belgrade, the capital of Serbia proper, through Brcko, Doboj, Gradacac and finally out, past Maglaj itself, to the sea.

Nearly a decade before, Maglaj had hosted the semi-finals of the European Basketball Championship; now it was so badly hit, and receiving so little media attention or aid that it was not clear who had survived inside the town. In the early autumn of 1992, a UNHCR officer in Zenica told me about Maglaj, twenty minutes north on the old highway. It had been under siege, surrounded on three sides, bombarded by Serbs since the summer before. Up until then, Maglaj had sustained seven air attacks by MIG-21s and JNA Eagles flying from the Serbian stronghold of Banja Luka, heavy artillery and sniping – the old town on the hill was practically levelled, there were no aid convoys getting in and the remaining inhabitants, no one was quite sure how many, were living underground in basements and shelters. The UNHCR officer thought that if I drove to the last Bosnian checkpoint outside Zenica, a commander might be able to help me get in, either by foot or by driving along the back roads.

It was hot, mid-October, airless, and stifling, when, accompanied by a photographer and an interpreter, I reached the last Bosnian command inside an old school on the road between Zenica and Zavidovici. The commander who met us gave us coffee, maps and advice: don't go to Maglaj. Since the Friday before, the city had been pummelled by the Serbs on the Ozren Mountains. The civilian casualties were heavy; the Armija was having difficulty sending reinforcements across the lines. There were recoilless guns on the hills and the front line was about one kilometre from the city centre. 'But the Serbs want Maglaj,' he said. 'They believe it is a Serbian republic.' Then he spoke to his assistant who brought in a young soldier, eighteen years old, who would lead us into Maglaj. On a piece of paper, he scrawled the name of the commander of the Armija in Maglaj, said he would radio ahead to the Bosnian first front line and wished us luck. 'Do not be frightened of the shells,' he said.

In the Lada Niva that we had rented in Split, the photographer drove and the soldier, who carried a photograph of his mother in his wallet, sat beside him. I was in the back, where I hated to sit because if something did happen I would not be able to get out quickly, next to Vesna Klanac, the Croatian journalist who was acting as our interpreter. We were holding hands, not talking because the photographer asked us please not to, as the car set off towards the final checkpoint before the race down the highway, the only road open, into Maglaj.

A Bosnian soldier waved us on, clearly confused: why were we going in when everyone inside wanted out? He told Vesna to follow the road and when we got about a kilometre ahead, to swerve to the right, avoiding the old town and the exposed centre where the gunners were targeting anything that moved. He said that fifty shells had fallen since 7 am, and that once we were inside Maglaj, we should not attempt to move around, but should stay underground because the gunners could see into the city. 'Once you are in,' he said, 'stay in the command and don't drive out until dark. Take the back road, around the mountain when you come out.'

In the car, Vesna fiddled with the flap on her flak jacket. We wore our helmets. I had my knapsack on my lap, perhaps thinking that if we had to dive out, I could take it with me – the torch, the apple I had bought a week before in Split, the bottle of water, the first aid kit.

The soldier was talking about his girlfriend, a Croat who had got out of Zenica. 'I haven't seen her in three no, six, months.' He opened his window and repeated the commander's words: 'Don't be frightened when a shell falls.' It took me a moment to notice that he did not say, Don't be frightened *if* a shell falls.

The first shell fell about thirty seconds later. The photographer ground the car to a halt, and then tried to drive around it. For a minute, there was pandemonium inside the Lada; the driver shouting at Vesna to ask the soldier what we should do – drive forward or stop the car – the soldier shouting and pointing to a dirt path off the road, Vesna trying to shout over the noise. A second shell came in: all I could see from the back was smoke and then I heard the thud. Within seconds we had driven off the highway, onto a dirt road, highway and we were out and running into a shelter.

It was cold and dank inside, there were refugees, frightened people sitting on piles of abandoned, wet clothes. My hands were shaking as I pulled out my cigarettes and my lighter; we sat in the middle of the room, away from the windows, and waited. We had gone too far to turn back to Zenica, but it was dangerous to move forward. After twenty minutes, we reluctantly got back into the Lada, the soldier holding his gun on his lap.

I don't remember much about that trip into the centre of town: maybe it took ten minutes, not even, but it felt like a lifetime because we all knew that we were being watched, that the fragile luck we had carried up until then could be broken. We found the command headquarters in the basement of a destroyed pizzeria, left the car and raced inside. There, the soldiers looked at us aghast: 'How did you get in?' No one had entered Maglaj for weeks; they could not believe that anyone would be so naïve as to try it. Outside the bunker, the heavy afternoon shelling was beginning.

One of the officers, who said he never drank, opened a bottle of brandy. 'Two months of constant shelling, do you know what that does to your brain?' Hamo Sukic, one of the officers, was playing with the cord of the field telephone that connected them with the front. 'You forget everything . . . what life was like, how people behaved before they turned into animals.' Then he took a call on the field telephone, listened and replaced the receiver. He looked at us, sitting silently drinking our slivovitz and smoking cigarettes, trying to push the adrenalin back so that our hands stopped shaking and our hearts stopped racing. 'The car behind you was not so lucky as you,' he said quietly. We got away, but they had taken the impact of the shell. Two people were killed; every time someone tried to retrieve their mangled bodies, they were pinned down by a sniper. So they were left lying in the road, the road that we had turned off.

The Bosnians had men, but no supplies. 'The biggest obstacle is the lack of arms,' said Herzog Slima, the deputy commander of the joint Muslim Croat forces in Maglaj, who had once spent a summer at Cambridge. 'When you think of the irony, all of our taxes went into funding the JNA, building up the Yugoslavian National Army which is now killing us. Then the fucking Chetniks [Serbs] took our arms.' He played with his glass. 'The only thing they can't take is our souls. We are going to hold out until they kill us all.'

We sat inside the bunker watching the commanders pore over their ancient maps until the shelling grew quieter and a soldier indicated that we could go above, but quickly, and only if we moved quietly, like ghosts through the streets. Outside the bunker, the city was sheathed in leafy stillness; odd how the trees were still blossoming even though Maglaj had been hit by thousands of shells. There was a pinball machine in the middle of the road and I stared at it, struggling to convince myself I was not in some surreal film set. There was no one on the street; Herzog Slima had said that there were only about 4,500 people left in the town, nearly 3,000 had fled in the past few weeks.

But there was someone in a garden, gathering windfalls and adjusting the sandbags in front of her shattered windows, preparing for the afternoon assault. She was called Seida, Seida Kadrebasic she said, introducing herself. She was 68 years old and lived alone in the house that had been her home for more than half of her life. When she had been given the chance to leave some months before, she had refused. Instead, she could stand in the garden, still flowering with the last of the summer roses and pause over her basket of mealy fruit, identifying the blasts that shook the trees: 'Light mortar, 60 mm, incoming,' she whispered and turned towards her house.

She was frail, but there was a sturdiness to her bones and her voice was rich. She had survived World War II, she reminded me, and she knew how to store food, how to keep a small bit of rice going for months, how to protect herself by moving all the furniture into one room and living there. Underground, in the cellar where she had been for two months since the heavy Serbian bombardment began, she had become accustomed to new sounds: multi-barrel rocket launchers; anti-aircraft guns; recoilless rifles. 'They launch everything here on us but atomic gas,' one commander in Maglaj told us. 'Last month they were dropping something like mustard gas that made us cough and our eyes hurt.'

The month before I arrived was the worst time in Maglaj: those were the days when the MIGs and the Eagles would fly overhead. Seida could hear them from her basement, lying on her bed, protected by her polythene bag stuffed with dirt. She started praying again in those months, she said, and sometimes, when her sister came to stay with her, sleeping on the sofa opposite the twin bed she had managed to drag down into the cellar, they would hold hands in the dark, the way they had when they were children, lying quietly, listening to the sounds of the shooting. 'You wait for the quiet so that you can sleep.'

In the summer, there was a time when she convinced herself that it would be quiet soon, that the war would end, that life would return to normal and she could leave the cellar. Then, gradually, she got used to the cellar and to the shelling and she decided that even though she was the only person still living on her lane, she would continue her routine: washing with the little bit of water left, squeezing her dresses and aprons with water and hanging them on the line in the garden before the morning bombardment began; searching for food in the overrun vegetable patch; storing as much wood as she could carry in the cupboard because what she feared more than anything, more than bullets or stray shrapnel, was dying slowly from the cold, alone in her basement.

In the afternoons she listened to Radio Sarajevo, scanning the messages from separated families, listening for news of her relatives. The sound drifted and echoed in the cellar: 'Family Cejvan from Kotor Varos. We are alive and in Travnik. Repeat, we are alive.' Where is my son? she would think, lying on the bed and folding her hands over her breast, as though she was at prayer, or deep in sleep. He was on the front line in the trenches above the hills; sometimes he came down and she fed him the rice, the apples, the beans that she would soak until they were soft. Oh my darling, my son, there is nothing I can do to protect you, to keep you alive. His wife and children had fled, months before, to Croatia, but Seida refused to leave as long as he was fighting. Maybe, she thought, I can keep him alive if he knows I am here, waiting in the valley below him.

Before I left her, she gingerly took me through the rest of the house, the rooms she had not lived in two months. 'I lived through the second world war,' she said. 'At least the shops were open and there were people on the streets.' In her sitting room, the books were burnt, the furniture pushed away from the windows, her grandchildren's toys still in place. There was no glass left in the windows. 'I don't know how to explain,' she said. 'The only way is to call it craziness. We lived together for so many years. Then they went to the mountains and started firing at us.' She led me out the back door and pointed in the direction of the hospital.

I was walking through the town with that Sarajevo walk, the paranoid twitch of the head, who's behind me?, stepping over shards of glass, hunks of metal, old car parts. The town had been completely and utterly trashed, and yet there was no sound because everyone was living underground. How many people were left? The UNHCR didn't know, neither did the Armija. Many of them would probably die anyway in a few months, either from the cold, starvation, or bullets. The temperatures were going to drop in the mountains to minus 20. At the height of the winter the snowdrifts could be nine feet deep.

Near the underground hospital was the Catholic church. The clock had stuck at 12, midday, the time the first air raid destroyed the reservoir, the water supply. The old part of town had been levelled. No one on the streets. The post office was destroyed, the tree in front of it splintered as though it had been struck by lightning. There was a bank and a sports hall, but nothing except the eerie pinball machine was left in the road.

In the marketplace the windows of the shops were smashed, the goods gone. My foot touched something and when I bent down to see what it was, I saw a photograph of a wedding couple, she in a long white dress, he in a suit, the edges of the picture burnt and the frame smashed. The fire brigade, the only

75

people who stayed above ground in Maglaj, warned me to get back to the cellar. This was the time of day that the shelling began. I ran to the hospital in the basement of an old apartment block. I knew where it was because there was a skip outside full of bloody bandages.

They got the wounded, civilians and military, and laid them on cots and tried to take out their shrapnel, tried to stop the blood and the oozing with the few bandages they had left. I knew there was blood in the bins outside even before I was close enough to see, because of the birds circling above.

All front line hospitals are the same: doctors in blood-spattered filthy coats and white clogs, the wounded lying on cots, embarrassed, not by their horrific wounds, the gaping holes in their flesh, but by their nakedness; the stumps of legs and arms, the smell of decay, the pounding outside even while you are standing in a place of healing. It was, one of the doctors told me, a slow day in Maglaj: by 2 pm, fifty wounded, two dead. 'I am a Muslim, but that is not important,' said Dr Fuad Pasic, who had been a doctor in the trenches for four months and had lost 15 kilos. His voice was soft, he spoke good English with a Bosnian accent. He was standing by the bed of a soldier, maybe twenty years old, no older, with his leg cut off just above the knee. 'Because this is a war between humans and inhumans. By the time they get some notion of what is happening to civilians, it will be too late. The West is accomplice to these war crimes.'

Maglaj hospital consisted of two rooms with cots pushed against each other holding sixty wounded civilians and soldiers. The hospital had been bombed out of many other places because as soon as the Serbs knew where it was they targeted it. But they had finally found two small rooms in the bottom of a block of flats. The doctors were short of antibiotics, plasma expanders, solutions for infusions, analgesics, spasmoradics, narcotics, anti-diabetic drugs ... 'Shall I go on?' Pasic said bitterly. He said he had been treating civilians suffering from the effects of noxious gases and from what he believed were napalm and cluster bombs.

'How do they intend to punish people for these crimes?' The man standing behind me also spoke good English. His face was deeply lined, emphasising prominent eyes. After his first front-line assignment, he had looked after men released from Omarska and Manjaca camps, men who came to him in the final throes of starvation, with bruises as big as watermelons on their backs from beatings, men who were throwing up blood, who could no longer shit anything but blood.

'Tell me something,' he said, bending over the man with half a leg. 'In 1981, there was a women's basketball tourna-ment. People from all over Europe came to Maglaj. Has the world forgotten us completely? Because locked away here, you have no sense of time, of reality. Outside, are they just passing resolution after resolution, or is somebody going to help us?'

Yasminka Smajilagic, half-Muslim, half-Serb, once had her office in the block of flats. A long, long time ago, before the war, twelve months ago, she had been a specialist orthodontist, fitting the children of the wealthy with metal retainers and braces to straighten their teeth. Now she was also underground, the only dentist left in Maglaj. Instead of fitting braces, Yasminka was yanking teeth from soldiers with no painkillers and an instrument (pliers, she called them) that she had salvaged when her office was destroyed. 'Believe me,' she said, 'I don't have a single tablet. It's hard because I used to be such a perfectionist and now I have the most primitive conditions, no light, only a torch.' She had never stitched a bullet wound or removed shrap-nel before the war, but now she could do it. Instead of risking the hospital, which was frequently targeted because the Serbs knew its position, soldiers sometimes came to her.

The soldier who was leading me through Maglaj that day had a toothache and we held hands and ran through the worst bit of the town, exposed to the snipers, to her house. When we neared the field in front of it, her husband, a gentle, sensitive man called Faruk who had been an electrical engineer, motioned for us to hurry inside, quickly. He was neatly dressed in a cardigan; later he told me that his greatest triumph was finding a small amount of water every day to shave; preserving his dignity was his little victory.

'Don't stand there,' he shouted. 'Run faster.' Yasminka had tried to get out twenty minutes earlier, had stood at the door leading down the stairs to the basement that had been her family's home for the last month, and had held her hand out as though she was testing the air. She had heard the sound of two explosions and backed down the stairs quickly.

It took a moment to get used to the dim light in the basement. There was a long table with a radio tuned in to Radio Sarajevo; they had been sitting listening to the news that Jajce was in flames. Six people lived in the room, sharing an ancient stove that had been re-activated at the beginning of the war; Yasminka's mother was knitting by the stove.

Yasminka was meticulous, even in the basement. She did not take money from her three patients a day, she did not have surgical gloves, but when a patient arrived, she made them sit at the table as she took down a careful case history. Her small range of equipment was laid out neatly on a table with a white cloth held down by mortar bases. Amar, her eleven-year-old son, acted as assistant, holding the torch over the mouth while Yasminka leaned over with her pliers, muttering. As the shells fell, she would yank a tooth. 'War is stupidity,' Faruk said, watching the operation. 'Nobody asked us if we wanted this war. Politics have nothing to do with ordinary people.'

'All I want,' said Yasminka, 'is for Amar to go back to school.

To get another guitar, to play instruments. To get ready for university.'

What she missed most was her freedom. The grand apartment she shared with her family on the north side of Maglaj was now gone. 'I took toothpaste, razors, some clothes and left everything else behind,' she said. 'Amar sneaked out later to get some toys.' The middle-class life, the easy days and nights, were gone. She had never washed clothes by hand before in her life; now it was the only way they could keep clean, if they waited for the water which arrived in town for only three hours in the morning. To bathe, a small pot had to be heated on the stove.

I left Yasminka because a runner arrived to tell me that I either had to leave town as soon as darkness fell, or stay for the next few days. The commander had heard that one of the soldiers behind enemy lines had intercepted a report: the Serbs were planning a major offensive that night which they believed would be the final push. The commander wanted us to go, because he could not guarantee our safety.

Yasminka was standing near the table, listening, even though the soldier, Vesna and I were talking in quiet voices. We gathered our things and when I left, I searched in my bag and pulled out my first aid kit which contained the most basic things: some plasters, a packet of aspirins, some Percodan, some army field bandages, some gauze and some vitamins, and gave it to her. She looked at me, threw her arms around my neck and burst into tears. Even now, I am ashamed of that moment because I could leave Maglaj, just get in a car and drive down the mountain path, but she could not, and I do not know what happened to her or her family. Because she was half-Muslim, half-Serb and her husband was Muslim, what she feared most was the Serbs entering the town. 'I still have hope,' she said, holding the first aid kit. 'Without hope you cannot live.'

Before I left, she made me take her only bottle of perfume

because she said she had no use for it. Her mother was standing next to her weeping. Faruk was solemn as he stood in the doorway, motioning us to run faster across the open space in front of their house. When I reached the pinball machine in the middle of the road, I looked back towards their door – they had gone down into the basement. It was a bad moment, like the times when I had left Klea and Mario and Marija and Sandra back in Sarajevo, got into a car and driven to the airport. I had the choice of coming and going; they were stuck forever, it seemed, in their basements.

We couldn't leave Maglaj until it was completely dark, and even then the commander was wary of letting us go. If we drove with the lights off, which we had to, the Serbs would still hear the engines of the cars. Earlier, when we had sat in the command and they had shared their food with us, he took me aside and thanked me for coming to Maglaj because no journalist had before. 'You cannot imagine what it is like,' he said, 'to know that someone from outside this place is listening.' Then he gave me a piece of paper with his name and the command's address:

> 'Herzog Slima
> Komanda Armija BiH
> Maglaj
> Republic Bosna i Hercegovina

He asked me to send him a copy of the story. I took the paper and wondered if he had gone mad, because he knew better than I did that it had been months since the postal system worked. Perhaps he was thinking that by the time we got out, the siege would be broken. Or maybe he was just upset by the phone call that had come through minutes before: the one screaming that the Serbs had nearly broken through the defences on the hills and had driven over three rows of trenches with their tanks. After the call, Slima dropped his head in his hands and said that he would find us a guide, soldiers that were from Maglaj and knew the back roads like the backs of their hands. Then he said goodbye, wished us luck, and went inside.

We found the guides, two local soldiers who drove ahead of us on the mountain paths in their rusted VW Golf. Even with them leading the way, one of us had to lean out the window and tell the driver how close he was to the edge because he couldn't see anything ahead of him or to the side of him, it was that dark and that quiet. And yet we weren't alone because the Serbs were very close, just above us on the hills.

If you come that close to knowing that at any second something might come down, you might lose your leg, your arm or worse, then you make a decision. Either you say you will never do it again, no more risks because you were stupid to get into it the first time, and lucky to get out, or you keep going because you think you've passed some weird initiation. We slept that night in an HVO barrack in Travnik, full of drunk and horny soldiers: we put our flak jackets against the door to keep them from getting in, getting near us, but that night I woke up to the sound of banging at the door. It was nothing, just a drunk coming back, but I couldn't sleep; instead I got up and walked to the broken window, dragging the sleeping bag with me. The moon was nearly full and the sky above Travnik was lit up. Some soldiers were standing guard outside the command. In the distance was the sound of machine-gun fire.

Throughout 1993 and into early 1994, Maglaj continued under siege, with one extended period when no aid was received at all. In the early part of 1994, the photographer Gary Knight and Martin Dawes of the BBC walked into Maglaj, since it had become impossible to drive in. Aid was coming in over the mountains by mule train. By that time, the Muslims had two enemies, the Croats and the Serbs. I wondered what had happened to Herzog Slima, who had assured me that the former alliance was indestructible. 'If anyone wants a good example of how Bosnian Croats and Bosnian Muslims get along,' he had boasted, 'they should come to Maglaj.'

But by the time Knight got there, that had all changed. He spent several days in the town and did not see Slima, or Yasminka, or her family. Whether they had got out or were dead, he did not know.

★

In the last week of October 1992, right as the weather changed and the cold began to come down from the mountains, we waited for the fall of Jajce. Near Prozor I saw a bus moving as slowly as possible up the hill: it was filled with very young soldiers and they were leaning out of the windows, waving, pressing their hands and their faces against the glass of the bus. On the side was a sign painted black: VOLUNTEERS FOR JAJCE. Vesna, standing next to me on the side of the road, shivered: 'They are so young,' she said quietly. 'And they are going to die. How can they ever survive Jajce?'

For weeks, Jajce had been poised to die. For five months, it had withstood a bloody, brutal siege, with reinforcement soldiers hiking in through the underwoods, and ambulances setting out every night from Travnik to bring out the dead and the wounded.

We were in Travnik, the ancient Ottoman town with the blue mosque, and as we waited cartloads of refugees were pouring down from the mountains, driven out of Jajce and the surrounding towns at gunpoint, flushed out of their homes, their farms, leaving behind the unburied and the dead. The refugees marched for days across the wet mountains, with their dogs, their children, their farm equipment. After they left, and after their houses had been looted, they could see the flames where the Serbs had ignited their homes.

In August, Ed Vulliamy, the *Guardian* correspondent who, along with ITN's Penny Marshall, broke the Omarska camp story earlier that summer, was part of a convoy of refugees that trudged across the mountains in April escaping ethnic cleansing near Sanski Most. He recalled the confusion and fear as the refugees walked for eleven hours, abandoning their belongings, their cars, and scurrying down mountain paths often only a few hundred feet from artillery positions. Oddly enough, Vulliamy would later recall the eeriness of silence: even the small children and babies seemed to sense the danger that they were in and clung to their parents.

Before Jajce fell on 30 October 1992, after five months of siege and fierce fighting, we heard that Kurt Schork from Reuters had managed to get in, driving at night. But when we met a British mercenary who agreed to take us in, we decided it was not worth the risk. Jajce was going to fall, it was only a matter of time, and we did not want to be inside when the Serbs took it. The defence of the city was maintained from Travnik, via a narrow 25-mile corridor that the Bosnians had carved through the wood and mountainside.

Later, we would hear a bitter version of the story of Jajce's fall from a Bosnian Muslim commander in Travnik. Towards the end, the Croats, who were still allied with the Muslims, had abandoned their trenches, leaving the Muslim fighters alone to man the lines, thus exposing the city to the Serbs. There were accounts of deals made between Radovan Karadzic and his Croatian counterpart, Mate Boban. Within hours of the Croats' desertion, Jajce had fallen to the Serbs and the Muslim fighters also fled. Some believe it was the first sign of the Serb-Croat collusion that would later explode in Central Bosnia. After the city fell, 7,000 Bosnians marched back to Travnik, bedraggled, confused, bitter. 'An army in retreat,' said one soldier miserably. The defeated soldiers had held the town for five months. But they had lost their front line. That was now at Karaula.

There were so many Jajce refugees flooding down the road from Turbe to Travnik, 30,000 of them, a column ten miles long, that the roads swelled like a scene from a Russian epic. One correspondent would later call it 'one of the most unforgettable days of the war', because the sight of so much suffering was almost unbearable. They carried their belongings on their heads, in their arms, and on carts pulled by ponies. As they walked, the Serbs shelled them from the hills; by the time they arrived in Travnik, they were exhausted and hungry, but beyond tears. The UNHCR, stretched beyond capacity, herded them into abandoned sports centres and schools but confessed that they had never seen such an exodus, so many people coming out of one place at the same time; forty or more of them to a room, lying on blankets all day waiting for their twice-daily bowl of rice, the only way of distinguishing one hour from the next.

Every morning, I drove into Travnik and went to the refugee centres and sat on the floor and listened to the stories: the women who had been raped by their neighbours, by men they had known all their lives who suddenly appeared on the door one day and forced them inside.

Wars centre around hospitals, because that is where the results can be seen. In the intensive care unit in Travnik hospital one morning, I heard a low primal moaning, like that of an animal, and when I found where it was coming from, I saw a twelve-year-old boy with his guts ripped open from below his chin to his pubic line, writhing on the bed in agony.

'Shrapnel wounds in the intestines,' said the doctor on call, lifting the sheet briskly. 'Trying to escape from Turbe with his family on a cart. No one can find his father. He's been alone here for nine days, no visitors and I only have enough painkillers to give him an injection once a day.' He was a Muslim, the doctor thought that he might have been hit by Croats, not Serbs – one of the first victims of the internecine fighting. Within three days, the doctor told us, fifty people had been killed in this new war.

The boy was lucid enough to tell me that his name was Salko Halep. He had a long thin face, grey eyes and lank, blondish hair that was plastered to his head with sweat. His mouth was gaping, open with pain. I sat by the bed thinking, please let this kid live. The next day when I came back he was in surgery, a nurse abruptly told me he would probably die: 'What do you expect?' she said, not unkindly, she was tired and overworked and had done, like the rest of the doctors, her share of 24-hour shifts. 'He barely has a stomach left.'

Salko did not die. One week later, I returned and he was still lying on the bed, but he was slightly less grey, his eyes were open and a man with a grizzled beard and filthy clothing sat next to him. His father. He had found Salko the day before and now the doctors were saying that he would live, that it would be a long time before he recovered fully, but he was drinking juice and could talk a little. The boy remembered nothing of the journey out of Turbe, the attack on his cart, or the trip to the hospital. He did not remember me sitting by his bed but he remembered his father coming into the room. He said he felt better. He asked me if I could find him some juice. Some do live.

On the way back to Split, driving over the mountains behind a truckload of drunken soldiers who kept firing at our heads, we stopped in a hospital in Tomislavgrad where the wounded soldiers from Jajce were being treated. An entire ward was full of young soldiers who talked about the last hours of Jajce, the houses burning, the entire city lit up like a Christmas tree, the rocketing, and then the HVO troops pulling out and leaving them on the front line. In one bed lay a young British soldier, a mercenary who had been in Jajce until the last days. 'We could have held out,' he said.

But the thing I remember about the fall of Jajce was this. There was a woman in one of the refugee centres, only thirty years old, called Bessima Behadzic. She had come down from Kljuc, a small village near Banja Luka, where she had been a farmer's wife. She had big strong bones and freckles, blonde hair and when she saw me she began to cry. In her hands, she had a small passport photo of a man, her husband, Sherif, who was also thirty and who had disappeared the summer before. One morning, Bessima had stepped out into her garden at 7 am and had seen the Serbs push her husband into a truck. 'I know he's alive, I know he's alive, please can you find him.' She pressed the photo into my hand, gave me his date of birth.

In Vitez, I gave the name to an aid worker. She took it and wrote it in a book marked 'The Disappeared'. The next week, I went back to see Bessima. An old woman was sitting in Bessima's place, on a rug in the middle of the room, with a small tin pot full of water.

'I'm going to walk over the mountains to find my son,' she said.

Vesna, who was translating, bit her lip. Another woman nudged her. 'She's gone crazy, don't listen to her.'

'Ask her where Bessima has gone.'

Vesna asked, there was a shrug. 'No one knows.' A crowd gathered around us and a small child was tugging at my hand. When I looked down I thought he would say 'bon-bon' and I had some in my pocket to give him. But he didn't, he repeated the phrase that all the children were saying that week, inside the refugee centre. Welcome to Hell.

THE CITY ON THE RIVER:

SPRING 1993

IN MAY, there was talk again of air strikes and that week someone went throughout Sarajevo hanging American flags and cardboard cut-outs of the Statue of Liberty on the walls of the smashed buildings. But no one believed the talk. Too much had happened, and too many people had died already to think that the West would intervene. Besides, America was preoccupied with domestic problems and Somalia. Why should anyone care about Bosnia? One of the waiters in the Holiday Inn said it was like a mountain shaking, but a mouse being born. 'Troops will never come here. There are big expectations, but nothing happens.'

Mustafa 'Talijan' Hajrulahovic, then the commander of the First Corps in Sarajevo laughed at the thought of the Americans dropping bombs on Serbian positions. 'Negotiations with the world community have amounted to nothing but world talk,' he said, playing with his thick moustache. 'They've already lost their authority by their lack of action; all we ask is for them to lift the arms embargo. It's in everyone's nature to want to defend yourself and your city.'

On the front lines, the soldiers who had been defending the city for a year were exhausted. They could listen to the radio and they knew that in town, people were beginning to go back to cafés and trying to live normal lives. For twelve months they had been sitting in trenches and they knew they were losing and they were exhausted.

'If anything was going to happen, it would have happened already,' said Mirza Sajanovic, a fighter from Stup. 'We feel abandoned and I believe, well most of us believe, that the war has taken on a new phase, an uglier one.'

We were in Stup early one morning. Cold, grey Sarajevo fog hung low; it was not yet summer. Mirza was smoking Sarajevo cigarettes, harsh cigarettes distributed free to the soldiers, wrapped in plain white paper. He exhaled a column of smoke.

'Now, the object is to destroy and separate.'

Colonel Jovan Divjac, a French-speaking Serb and a commander in the mainly Muslim Bosnian Army, laughed at the thought that the war might be over. 'The Serbian side has not finished yet,' he said. 'They have not created the steps to make Greater Serbia.' There was more coming, he said, far worse than had been already. He reminded me that there was still fighting in Sarajevo, Central Bosnia, in Gradacac, Maglaj, Vitez. There were forty tanks attacking Brcko, a city strategic to the Serb-desired northern corridor. But the greatest tension of the war had resulted from the Vance-Owen Plan, unveiled in January 1993, which had threatened the fragile unity between Muslims and Croats in Central Bosnia. In Vitez, the Croats and Muslims, former allies, had turned on each other as the Muslims braced themselves to take the Croatian pocket, which under the plan would go to the Croats. In his office in Sarajevo, Jovan Divjac contemplated the fate of the plan. 'My dear,' he said airily, 'do not forget that there is now fighting in Central Bosnia between the Muslims and the Croats. It is a new dimension to the war.'

Mostar, the ancient Ottoman city, had always been a flashpoint. Before the war its population was neatly divided between Croats, Muslims and Serbs. It was only a matter of time before it exploded. In early May, the Croats began a campaign of terror, first driving the Muslims out of the west side of the city, pushing them to the east side, and then bombarding them with rockets, mortars and sniper bullets. It was a clear attempt to destroy a civilian population; they had learned their lesson very well from the Serbs.

Now the Bosnian Muslims had not one enemy but two.

★

I slept at night on the east side of the Neretva River in Mostar, in an apartment owned by Orhan, the General's son. He was 21 years old, with an upturned nose, wide brown eyes and freckles. When he took me to the front line less than 10 metres from the apartment where five of us slept, he sprinted like a kid. He wore a surfer's bracelet, a piece of multi-coloured yarn, for good luck, a bandanna wrapped around his right wrist, camouflage trousers, too big, and Nikes. He had a gun his father had given him, which, when he looped it under his arm, looked oddly out of place.

He wanted to be a journalist if the war ever ended, or a musician. At night, when the heaviest battles began, and the soldiers began exchanging heavy machine-gun fire across the river, from the right to the left bank and back again, we sat in the dark and drank Loza brandy and he played 'Until the End of the World' by U2 on a small tape recorder. We listened to the same tape over and over until his sixteen-year-old sister Alma got frightened by the shelling so close to the window and began to think that maybe the sound of the music could carry across the river. The Muslims still held the river, but the front line was separated by a road which was no-man's-land. The soldiers were 40 metres apart, could see each other's heads or guns. If you saw a head opposite, you never looked closely because it could be a face you knew: someone you went to school with, someone you played soccer with, someone who lived next door.

When the batteries on the tape got slow, we sat in darkness. Orhan talked then about going to London, becoming a student, forgetting Mostar, the war, being a Muslim, growing up in Bosnia, Yugoslavia, everything. He smoked some dope mixed with tobacco and we listened to the sound of the mortars. When I stood too close to the window, Alma got agitated and fiddled with the gold fleur-de-lys that hung on a thin chain around her neck, the symbol of Bosnia. The last time her father had gone to Sarajevo, to lead fighters out of the capital and into Mostar via the secret underground tunnel, he had wandered into Bascarsija, the Old Town, where the old jewellery and *cevapcici* shops were shuttered and closed. Somehow he found one of the gold merchants and convinced him to open his shop, bought the necklace for his only daughter, who, even though it was a war and life was shit, was still a teenager and still wanted to be pretty. So he bought it and had it wrapped in tissue paper. He carried it back in his pocket and when he finally got back to the East Bank, having led his men through the mountains outside Sarajevo, through Jablanica, and finally, across the front lines into East Mostar, he gave it to Alma and she burst into tears. 'In the middle of war, in the middle of leading soldiers, he brought me a present.'

After the Loza there was nothing else to do. Orhan and his best friend, Robert, were on early shift on the front line the next morning. The General was somewhere on the front; Orhan had not seen him in a week.

'Where is he?'

Shrug. 'Who knows? Some apartment, somewhere.' He said it sarcastically, but his face, with the freckles and upturned nose, was bitter. 'It's been a long war ... my father has many lives, works hard ... knows he can die like that ... ' He snapped his fingers. His mother, a child psychologist, was trapped on the other side of the river. If he stood by the windows, now blown out and replaced by plastic, and if Alma didn't get too nervous, he could point roughly in the direction, across the river, where she might be. 'If she is still there, if she is still alive.'

We ate some bread and cheese that Philippe, the French journalist who was with me, had carried into Mostar in his Eastpak, and some tomatoes, the first ones Alma had seen for months, that we had bought in Citluk, a village on the Croat side. That was where we had found the abandoned road that led us to the east bank. Orhan ate nothing because he had eaten rice at the barracks and the past few weeks since the heaviest fighting began his stomach was always in a tight clenched knot; it was impossible to eat if you thought you might be shot at any time. Then we went to bed, but when I lay down on the narrow twin bed it was too loud to sleep, the fighting was too close. In the next room, Robert was singing James Brown's 'I Feel Good' in English and Orhan, on the sofa next to him, was laughing. When I finally did fall asleep hours later, I left the small window open and was awakened by a bullet hitting the building next door.

In the first light of morning in Mostar, the sun was already high and I remembered what my guidebook to Hercegovina said. In the summer, Mostar was the hottest place in the former Yugoslavia and, aside from the island of Hvar, the sunniest. The streets were full of people who had slept outside, in the gutters. In the park turned cemetery the headstones were all marked with the names of fighters born in the early seventies who had died in 1993. 'The object of this eruption, of this hatred and animosity,' the Seid Smarjic, the mufti for all of Hercegovina, told me, 'is for the Croats to destroy everything which is Muslim. And that includes the ancient mosques.'

The smell of shit on the street and ripe trash was overwhelming; there were bloody bandages in the bins outside the hospital, covered in flies and always there was the sound of someone crying: not necessarily the children, who tended to run through the streets and crowd in the park opposite the Armija headquarters, carrying guns clumsily carved from wood, but the parents, huddled in the gutters, stopping anyone they thought could help them get away from the east bank, get to somewhere else. As I walked by, someone would stand up and block my way.

'Please, can you take my daughter out of Mostar? She's only four. I want her to live.'

'Can I have a cigarette? Please, a cigarette!'

'I want to talk to you. Please sit with me. I have an important story.'

'Take me across the river, please take me with you.'

In the park near the shelled mosque, a man about my age was kneeling on the ground, holding a bunch of flowers. Where, in the middle of the siege, had he managed to find flowers?

'You speak English? Deutsch? French? Can you get a message for me to my wife in Split? I haven't spoken to her since this began.'

I knelt beside him and began to write her name, her number, but before I finished, his eyes shifted and he stood up. A water truck had rolled into town and before the snipers on the other side realised it was there, the people ran to it, clutching water bottles and buckets in a kind of frenzy.

One year before, the Muslims and Croats had fought together in Mostar against the Serbs in the hills: together they had liberated Mostar from two months of bombardment and part-occupation by the Serbs. They had driven them across the Neretva in June 1992, across to the old town on the east bank, and up into the mountains. Then the Vance-Owen Plan sent the factions into turmoil, trying to carve up as much territory as they could in as short a time as possible. The Croats wanted Mostar, believed it to be the spiritual and cultural capital of Herceg-Bosna, the mini-state within Bosnia that they were crudely trying to create. The alliance signed in July 1992 between the Bosnian Muslim forces and the Bosnian Croat forces for a joint military and political front meant nothing in the race to take land. The Croats had their own army, the HVO, which was better equipped than the Muslims – better armour, better weapons and 1,000 kilometres of coastline to get supplies in. The Muslims were landlocked. To get reinforcements out of Sarajevo, still under siege, they had to cross through a secret underground tunnel and then over front lines, through the mountains.

And so, one year later, the strong turned on the weak in the push for Mostar and edged them into the old town. More than betrayal, there was confusion. In Mostar those weeks, everyone had a glazed, manic look in their eyes, the look of people who knew that they were going to die. There was no space to move on the streets, there were people moving quickly everywhere: on Marsala Tito street, near the hospital, near the park. If you could see the river from where you were standing, you were in a bad place, and you held your breath and ran.

No one knew how many people were trapped in East Mostar. The Armija, the defending Bosnian Army composed largely of Muslims, claimed 35,000, but the Red Cross thought it was closer to 30,000. Zijo Suljevic, the director of 'logistics' during the siege, said there were close to 40,000 people, 5,000 of them new refugees who had walked across the river or the mountains since the fighting began. Before the war, he said, there were around 20,000 people in the area.

30,000 bodies on a piece of land one mile long and 300 yards wide, with something like 350 more people crossing the bridges each night, bussed over by the Croats who were pushing them off the west bank. Mostly, they were living on the streets; the luckiest ones managed to find a chair in the abandoned cinema.

There was Zoria, a 35-year-old woman from Bosanski Brod, who had been displaced the previous July by Serbs; who had then spent the next nine months moving from town to town in Central Bosnia looking for a safe place. She got to Mostar in mid-April, settled on the west side, then the fighting broke out and her sixteen-year-old daughter was wounded by shrapnel and taken away by doctors. One morning, the soldiers came, took Zoria away from the flat she was sharing with ten strangers, and brought her across the river. She stayed inside the cinema most days, only leaving to get her litres of water from the Red Cross, then coming back, sitting in one of the faux-plush chairs in the abandoned cinema, rocking back and forth.

There was an old man sitting on the floor; he only had one hand but he was holding a transistor radio, trying to tune it in to a station that no longer existed. He told me his name: Mustafa Culesca. He was 62 and he had been ethnically cleansed twice: once by the Serbs, once by the Croats. He had been in Mostar for four months. He had lost his wife, his father and his brother. 'My mother died when I was four years old,' he said dreamily, still touching the radio knobs. 'It was a different war then.' He turned back to the radio, barely looking up when a shell landed near the cinema.

After the sniping, the shelling and the rocketing, the biggest problem was lack of water (there was no pump, only a free pipe, and the Red Cross could only allot one and a half litres of water per person a day to wash and cook), followed by disease and hunger. Only two convoys had got into East Mostar since 9 May, when the fighting began. For weeks, no convoys had crossed the river and the people had finished their stocks of potatoes and tinned meat; now they were eating the cherries from the orchards that were close to the Serbian front line. Everyone reminded you, pointing with their fingers and motioning with their eyes, of the two enemies. On one side were the stony Podvelezje

Mountains, and behind them the Serb positions and the front lines further east; on the other side of the river, the Croats.

In Medjugorje, twenty minutes down the road, the Croats sold religious trinkets, plastic rosary beads, velvet framed paintings of the Virgin Mary, who was said to have appeared to three teenagers in 1981. In between plugging the tourist industry, they blocked the aid the relief organisations were trying to ship to East Mostar. 'It's a mess, an emergency,' said the UNHCR spokeswoman who had also overseen the evacuation of Srebrenica one month before, but who was now overcome with frustration and rage. 'They are effectively encircled, there's a shortage of food, there are prisoners ... and we are still in the process of finding out exactly what is happening there.' She stared at her desk, and played with a piece of paper. 'A mess.'

In the hospital, Amila, a tall blonde doctor who would give birth later that year, sat on a dirty bed rubbing her head with fatigue and frustration. The body of a man in his early thirties, killed by a sniper that morning was lying on a cot in the hallway. No one had covered him yet, but his year of birth was printed on a card: 1963.

Amila spoke in short, choppy sentences, gulping the cigarette I had given her between breaths. Thirty dead since the fighting began ten days ago on 9 May, 400 wounded. No blood, no plasma. Seven specialist doctors, no instruments until the ICRC (International Committee of the Red Cross) managed to get in. Forty patients, crowded into the old library now being used as a hospital, books and pictures of Tito over makeshift beds, legs blown off at the knee, arms shot up, eyes blinded by shrapnel, men screaming in pain and the entire place stinking of death. Children staring straight ahead. A woman, or not really a woman, a teenager, lying naked on her stomach on a dirty bed; her back and buttocks bare, her dressings being changed, one delicate, barely grown-up leg cut off just above the knee.

Amila was watching, not really seeing, her brain working on autopilot, just going through the motions in a kind of exhausted, brain-dead state, but still moving her hands, her fingers cutting bandages, checking pulses, filling syringes. 'Mine is a simple story,' she said. She had worked in a big hospital on the west side before the war. At 5 am on 8 May, she had woken up and heard the first shots. She sat on the edge of her bed and tried to think, because she knew that those shots had not come from their old enemy, the Serbs, but from the Croats.

'And now, everyone says that here in East Mostar, we are like a little Sarajevo.' She pushed her thick hair out of her face and held it behind her head in a ponytail. Her white coat was splattered with blood, there were purple circles under her eyes. 'But we are not like Sarajevo, because we don't have one enemy. We have two.'

Outside the Armija headquarters, I met an Englishman who was training Muslim fighters. He was 58, a former British Army Airborne sergeant, from Middlesex, who had left the HVO, the Croatian Army, in the autumn of 1991, during the height of the war in Croatia. He was one of a number of international mercenaries sent to train Croats near Grude in Hercegovina. Then, in October 1992, shortly before the first Muslim-Croat internecine fighting broke out near Prozor and Vitez, he was sitting in a meeting near Medjugorje when he realised that the Croats were planning to make a deal with the Serbs to carve up Bosnia. 'I remember one of the HVO commanders saying that up to one million people would die, but it was not our problem.' He left shortly afterwards, crossing over the lines at night to join the Muslim side. 'Because one side, the Muslims, are fighting for survival, the other, the Croats, are fighting for territory,' he said. 'Not for themselves, but for Croatia.'

Before Yugoslavia, he had served in thirty wars as a mercenary, he said, the longest in Beirut, but, he said, 'This is the first job, this place, Mostar, I ever had where I lost money. This war is dirty, aimed at civilians. The Serbs targeted these people and now the Croats. It's just a terror campaign against civilians.'

He had tattoos embedded on the fingers of both hands: HATE and LOVE. He had been on the east bank for some time; training the kids, as he called them, without the benefit of arms or artillery. Teaching these soldiers who used to be tour guides, students, dentists and architects, how to behave like guerrilla fighters.

The Croats paid him ten pounds a month during the war in Croatia, the Muslims did not have anything to give him. I was wary because there were many mercenaries in Bosnia that year who had come because they liked to kill. I met some in Travnik during the fall of Jajce who crossed over Serb lines at night and slaughtered front-line soldiers. But this one said he was different. He had experience and once he realised the Croats were planning to slaughter the Muslims, he ran away to join the other side, because, he said, he was able to tell right from wrong. He didn't have a passport or money. In his wallet he still had his British driving licence. If the Croats found him, if they overran the east bank the way everyone expected them to at any point, they would kill him. He had already heard his name on their radio; he was desperate to get out of the east bank, but there was no way out.

With Philippe, I had discovered a back road into the east bank, through Croat lines. It was a route the UN military observers in Medjugorje showed us on a map one drunken night, a bit doubtfully, because they were not sure how many mines there were, and exactly where the snipers were, but they thought it was safer than the route we had taken in the unarmoured Lada

Niva that occasionally stalled: straight across the Neretva, on a shaky wooden bridge from Croat territory onto the east bank. I hated that trip, sat next to Philippe wearing my flak jacket and helmet; but he did not wear his because he said it was easier to drive. In those maybe four minutes that it took to pass from safe area to exposed area, knowing that the snipers were watching us, there was a feeling of losing control. When that happens, there is nothing you can do but wait, or close your eyes.

After we had helped the British mercenary escape to Split, and eventually to England, Croat soldiers told a contact in Split that they had known exactly what we were doing all along. 'Tell your friends the journalists,' he said, 'that we had them targeted with an RPG as they crossed the river. But we decided to give them a break.' Later that summer there was a rumour amongst the press corps that the Croats, angered by what they saw as the journalists' propaganda, had put a 50 DM price on their heads.

The mercenary knew the commanders and led us inside the Armija headquarters, dank, dark, filled with soldiers coming from the front and shifting positions: exhausted, dirty clothes, muddy sneakers, ancient guns. The atmosphere inside the building was not tense but terrified. 'They're doomed,' he said. 'Everyone feels it, no one admits it. How long do you think this can last? They don't think they will be the winners, because there are no winners.' He shook his head. 'The UN has a lot to answer for. How many people have been killed that did not have to die?'

The Armija headquarters were frequently hit, you could not stand near the windows or walk out on the terrace. The commander, Midhad Hujdor, had been up all night on the river, and was slumped in a chair. At 5.30 am, when he had thought he would be able to sleep, the shelling had started: rockets, tanks, mortars. Upstairs, he was sitting at a long table and playing with a Bic lighter, but he stood up when we entered. 'No coffee, sorry.' He stared at me. 'We can't stop it. For how long, we can't stand it, but there's no way to surrender. Until they kill us all. We're going to die anyway, either by ethnic cleansing, or we die by fighting.'

They were fighting without many resources. According to one commander, they had lost around eighty fighters since the offensive began. They had one brigade of 1,800 men, composed of an anti-tank unit, an anti-sniper unit and guerrilla fighters. There were 142 men on the front lines. Across the river, 40 metres away, in their positions in the new bank and the school, the Croat fighters had an estimated six brigades.

'During the first battle,' said one soldier, 'we realised we were completely surrounded and sealed in on four sides. Three by the HVO, one by Serbs.' They believed their fate was simple: first the heavy artillery attacks, then the death squads. 'It's the Balkan mentality,' he said, and led me to the anti-tank unit, a group of men positioned in a school fighting off Croat tanks with old hunting rifles. They gave me cherries that someone had picked, and wanted to give me the last of their coffee, and to demonstrate their most sophisticated weapon: an old hunting rifle fitted with a grenade. 'But we have a triumph today,' cheered the commander. 'We hit a tank today.'

In the Armija headquarters, Esad Humo, a deputy commander, in his former life an architect, said, 'The Bosnian Croats are using Croatia as a base, they have money and guns from there. The Bosnian Serbs are using Serbia as a base. We only have ourselves, and an arms embargo. No way to get soldiers in or out of this place, no way to get guns. We're surrounded on all sides, but if they want us to fight, we will fight for ourselves. We'll use up all the ammunition that we have and after that,' he smiled slightly, not showing his teeth, 'we will use stones.'

The mercenary introduced me to S., a 35-year-old Croat who

had refused to leave the east bank and was fighting with the Muslims. He was, according to the mercenary, the best shot the Bosnian Army had. So far he had killed fifty people on the other side with his 7.2 calibre bullets that could hit someone one kilometre away. His team of three men, called the anti-sniper unit, had so far killed 116 Croat snipers, shooting 43 in the head and 73 in the heart.

S. had lived in Sarajevo for twenty years and did not understand the war. He was a Croat, fighting with a Muslim army, killing other Croats. He said he was fighting with them because they were the good guys, that he would never shoot Croat civilians, that he would only shoot other snipers. 'I don't hate Croats,' he said. 'I fight for the people who need help.' He wore red sneakers, a black headband, a peace sign around his neck and a heart tattoo, but when I joked that the heart meant love, he stared straight ahead. 'There is no love anymore,' he said. 'Only war.'

Outside the headquarters, there was a crazy man shouting at the soldiers passing him on the narrow street.

'If Islam does not bring clean bodies, the world will be destroyed by illness,' he shrieked. 'French kings never took a bath. The West will crash down next year. Some big men from the East will destroy the West. America will be destroyed by AIDS.'

S. stared at him. 'This is Apocalypse now!' he shouted. Someone next to me spat. 'Fundamentalist.'

Jasmin Gostevic, a 23-year-old fighter, was leaning against the wall smoking a cigarette, bare to the waist, his thin torso deeply tanned by days manning the front line. Before the war, he was the town's most famous tour guide and rode through the streets on his Vespa. Now he was a sniper. 'This will be a Bosnian Vukovar,' he said and the mercenary, who was sitting on the corner watching him, shook his head.

'It's all madness, madness, madness,' he said. 'It's like being in Hell.'

Stari Most, the fifteenth-century bridge that symbolised Muslim ethnicity, was still standing in the early days of the siege. By mid-May 1993, it had been hit six times – four times by Croats, twice by Serbs – and sandbags hung over the sides in a futile attempt to protect it from any more shelling. On the top, a blue and white Bosnian flag was stretched. It was a defiant gesture because sooner or later the Croats would level it with their heavy artillery. To them, Mostar was the capital of Hercegovina. It was a Croat city, and they wanted it back without any traces, any remnants, of its Muslim past.

'Why target that mosque, that bridge?' Nerkez Mackiz, a 56-year-old Muslim civil engineer, former professor at Mostar University, said, as he waited in a deportation centre in no-man's-land. The room was crowded: people waiting with pitiful sacks, remnants of their lives: a bag of food, some towels, some winter clothes although outside it was hot. 'That bridge has survived attacks from the Venetians. And the mosque – what have they done to the mosque! It is 500 years old, it survived two world wars, and now it is a pile of bricks. It took this kind of hatred to bring it to the ground.'

Because he was a civil engineer, Nerkez knew things about that bridge: that when the Turks took over Mostar in the fifteenth century, it was a wooden bridge suspended on chains; that later, in the sixteenth century under Suleyman the Magnificent, the construction of the bridge had begun. It was finally finished in October 1557, designed by Hayrudin, a student of Sinan, the famous Turkish builder. It was 28 metres long, nearly five metres wide and had a single stone arch. In the summer, it was about 20 metres above water level. Built on the narrowest part of the Neretva, the bridge became the symbol of Mostar – around it the town developed, its towers, gates, mosques. Now it was a target caught between two front lines.

Nerkez was sitting on the floor, his arms wrapped around his legs. At his feet were two bags: one containing some food, the other some clothes. The night before, he and his wife had found a door to sleep on the seventeen nights before that, they had slept on the floor. His documents were gone, he had no passport, and he was aware that purely on the basis of the spelling of his name, there were places in his country he could never go to again. 'I have a Muslim name,' he said. 'But I never go to the mosque. Does this mean we have to leave our homes, because of this?' He did not know where he was going. This was his second 'ethnic cleansing'; he had already been cleansed from his beautiful house in the best district in Mostar by the Serbs.

He talked about the start of the war in Yugoslavia, when 'several years ago, some republics wanted to share the country . . . it has now come to this.' His friends from Mostar had begun leaving as early as 1991, taking their things and going to America, London, but he had waited because, like most people, he thought it would pass. Besides, there was their weekend house on the Dalmatian coast, their boat; their eldest daughter was studying piano, she had been given an award as the best student piano player in the former Yugoslavia. They waited, not really believing anything would happen. His family had lived in Mostar for 400 years. He was a professor. His wife was a judge. They had money, culture, connections, he had worked in England, in America. What could harm them? Then, so quickly, within a matter of weeks, they were fighting outside his doorstep and it was too late, the house was raided at 5 am, and the only things they managed to take were some clothes and, oddly enough, some hats. 'You don't know what you're thinking when that happens, your whole life flashes before your eyes.' They were pushed out, first by the Serbs, then by the Croats, now they were waiting for a convoy so that he and his wife, Mulija, could be part of a cattle car that was called a 'civilian exchange'. He was finally leaving Mostar, his city on the river, but he did not know where the bus would take him.

'Listen. Before the war, there were things in this town, the aluminium industry, the aeroplane industry, the hydroelectric plant, and there were people – Muslims, Serbs, Croats, gypsies, Jews lived together without any problem. We used to have a university of all nations. Now, the government wants to install a university solely for Croats. They want the national language to be Croatian, not Bosnian. Can you imagine the Croatian language in a town that is 70 per cent Muslim? We understand each other perfectly well, but that is nationalism.' He stared at the ground. 'And what happens now, is that anger grows, anger grows up. We must change ourselves.'

The family was scattered because Muslims were forbidden to travel to Croatia, and the children had left before the heavy fighting began. One fifteen-year-old son was in Split, studying the violin. Another daughter, who had also finished her middle school diploma in music, had been studying civil engineering. The eldest, his 24-year-old daughter, was studying in Novi Sad, in Serbia, and her parents did not even know if she had got her degree. She had been stranded there for more than eighteen months, could not find her way home.

Nerkez said that he had aged twenty years in the past three weeks. 'And we don't know anything about the future. It's like an illness, a terrible illness, we are occupied all the time with this. We don't know where we are going, but we don't worry because we have nothing left here.'

As Nerkez was driven from the east bank, over the Neretva for what he thought was the last time, his last image of Mostar was of Stari Most.

★

That night, when the sun had just set, the mercenary took us to the first front line near the river. We started in an abandoned shop, drank two glasses of Loza, and then I put on my flak jacket and ran with Orhan, Robert, Philippe and Jasmin between the buildings down to the river. We ran in a single file across paths through the woods, where maybe one year before children built tree houses. Orhan was in front of me, he would take my hand when we reached a wall or had to jump across some rocks; the mercenary was in the lead and, for some reason, getting agitated. He came close to us and said that when we got to the river, we must stay close to the buildings. When I followed Orhan away from the buildings, the mercenary stopped us and whispered fiercely: Listen to me if you want to stay alive. Orhan, who had been vaulting like a young deer through the trees, kicked a rock defiantly.

We came to an abandoned apartment block. The first front line. There were soldiers crouched behind it, or not really soldiers, kids, actually, dressed in dirty fatigues that somebody gave them, with handguns instead of Kalashnikovs. They took cigarettes gratefully and curled into their blankets. One of them was wearing slippers, felt slippers, and listening to a Walkman.

It was dark, and we could not use torches, so we waited until our eyes adjusted and then began to move quickly, running through the trees, the branches snapping in our faces, and then moving through a series of interconnecting basements on the Muslim front and there ahead was the Croat front line, with the shadowy heads of their soldiers, their artillery, their guns. Then we went through another door, expecting to find another abandoned hovel filled with Muslim soldiers, but no – it was a frightened family huddled in the darkness, nine of them in a tiny room, cowering because they did not know who was bursting in this time. We stopped, amazed.

They were living, literally, on the front line. When they saw we were not going to hurt them, the terror slowly ebbed from their faces.

'We weren't going to leave our homes,' said one of the women in perfect English. 'And now it's too late. My God, do you have a cigarette?'

She had been there for two weeks, with her children, her mother, her aunts, her neighbours. Before the war, she had been a teacher, she had studied in Sarajevo, she knew the same people I knew, she had been a student of Mario Susko's. Her name was Snerja, which she told me translated as Snow White.

'Welcome to Wonderland,' she said, trying to smile.

When I left Mostar in early June, I hugged Alma, then Orhan. He was thin underneath his green t-shirt: bony shoulders, concave chest, sinewy arms.

I looked hard at him, wondering when I would see him again, if I would, and I said, 'Stay alive', something I had heard soldiers say to each other before they went off to Jajce in Central Bosnia the autumn before.

'You too. See you in London.'

We both laughed, because we knew it would never happen. Philippe, who was waiting in the Lada Niva with the engine running, shouted at me to get moving because I was standing in the sniper line, and I had one last look at Orhan: a kid with a surfer bracelet and freckles. We climbed into the Lada Niva, I put on my helmet, opened the window, and Philippe told me to put on the seatbelt in case something happened and he got shot and the car went out of control. I shook my head because the seatbelt made me feel claustrophobic and I would rather jump out of the car if something happened. In the West Bank in Israel I had never worn a seatbelt because if a molotov is thrown in the window, you could get burnt alive. I was terrified of getting rocketed as we crossed the bridge.

We screeched out of the alley behind the General's apartment, in view of the snipers. They shot at us right away, missed, Philippe said, 'Merde', and drove faster. We drove out the most direct but dangerous way, straight over the bridge, Philippe swearing and me with my eyes closed and my fists clenched.

He drove so fast over the river that he couldn't turn in time when we reached the end of the bridge and, as we edged into Croat territory, he slammed into a lamppost. My head hit the dashboard, but I had on my helmet, so I was alright, Philippe jammed his knee against the wheel. We staggered out and checked the damage: nothing, and then laughed with relief. The Croat soldiers who had watched us cross the river, obviously having decided not to shoot us, looked at us in disgust and gave us directions to the Croat headquarters.

Inside the 'Assistant for Information and Propaganda', Mr Jago Musa, grudgingly decided to speak. He said that the Croats did not want to see the city of Mostar divided but, according to the Vance-Owen Plan, Mostar was designated the capital of province number eight – Croat territory. 'But the Muslims refuse to accept the Vance-Owen Plan,' he said, waving his hand, as though he was surprised by their audacity. 'It is their fault.'

Then he pointed to a map and said the population of Mostar before the war was 40 per cent Muslim, 40 per cent Croat and the rest mixed. 'But the real problem,' he said, his eyes shifting uneasily, 'are the refugees that came down from the mountains and flooded our city. All of them are Muslims.' His voice rose. 'We are under attack also. We gave them weapons. We gave them artillery. This is not a fight between Croats and Muslims, it's a fight against politics coming from Sarajevo. They want to mask it as democracy, but it's not.'

And what of the 1,800 Muslims being held by Croats in the

former JNA barracks, in an act which the UNHCR had described as 'significant . . . the first organised arrest of inhabitants on the west bank'? What about the people who were taken, according to the UNHCR reports, at first light. Rounded up by the HVO soldiers who stormed their flats, took them at gunpoint, moved them onto buses and drove them to Rodac, to the Heliodrom? What happened to those men, women and children? Their homes were looted. Their houses were burnt down. 'Many of them had been citizens of the west bank for twenty or more years,' A UNHCR spokesman had told me earlier in the week. Two hundred of them that week had been bussed out by Croats.

Wasn't that ethnic cleansing? What about the Muslims' claim that 800 fighters were missing, that those men were being held in basements, houses, cellars in West Mostar?

Musa's eyes shifted. 'They are not prisoners. They are there so that we can protect them.' But when I started to argue that that was precisely what the Serbs had told journalists the summer before when men from the Prejidor region suspected of being 'Muslim extremists' were discovered inside Omarska prison, tortured and beaten, Musa held up his hand and his face closed down like a gate. 'I know what you think of us,' he said. He shouted for his secretary and asked me to leave.

In Medjugorje, in a small pristine pilgrims' hotel, I filed my copy over the telephone, reading quietly while the massive Croat hotelkeeper glared at me, until the copytaker in London broke in.

'We're being tapped,' she said nonchalantly. 'Hang up the phone and let's start again.' She phoned back; we repeated the process three times until we worked out a system to transcribe the names of people on the east bank I was writing about. It took two hours. I spoke to my desk at the *Sunday Times* and told them I would file the names tomorrow. When I finished, the hotelkeeper was still watching me from behind the desk.

I smiled politely and reached for my key. He glared. 'We are Christians,' he said. 'They are not. We once lived together but we don't anymore. Death to all Muslims.'

I stared at him to see if he was joking. His face was twisted in a grimace. He repeated his words as he handed me the key to my room, one that had a crucifix hanging over the bed and a Bible on the table. 'Kill all Muslims.'

The next day the telephone was closed for international calls. 'May I phone my office?' I asked politely.

'No,' he replied in an equally polite voice. The UNHCR, whose phone line was also tapped constantly, let me use theirs.

I drove to Split through the heart of Hercegovina, stopping along the way to talk to the Croat nationalists in Grude, angry men who felt the world's press had turned on them but who would not talk about the Heliodrom or give us access to the prisoners. Then I left for Split and ate dinner in a hotel spray-painted with graffiti: ALL FOR CROATIA. It was impossible to feel objective when it was clear that, at least in Mostar, the Muslims were trapped between two enemies. That night, I had terrible, paranoid dreams: that the Croats read my copy and sent Ustasha terrorists after me. When I woke up, there was a man in my hotel room, rifling through the papers on my desk. I rubbed my eyes, and began to scream.

He turned, opened the door that I had locked before I fell asleep, and ran down the hall. I locked my door again, and two hours later, was woken up by more screams: he was a thief, maybe a refugee, the management said, but he had run out past the policeman at the gates of the hotel, and into the town. How do you know he's a refugee? I said. They shrugged.

The next day, I flew back to Sarajevo on a Hercules crowded with pallets of rice and macaroni, not talking to the two other journalists who sat next to me in their flak jackets and their helmets. Sarajevo had changed in the three weeks I had been gone, or maybe it was just that I had come from a compressed version of the siege, a place where there was no black market because there was no money, no supplies, no anything. In Sarajevo, it seemed everyone wanted something – cartons of cigarettes, chocolate, whisky, press cards. In Mostar, even though the desperation was greater, people did not grab, perhaps because they had not been desperate for long enough, perhaps because they felt their fate was sealed, that they were in fact doomed.

But they did manage to stay alive. Sometime later that month, a journalist from NBC went to Mostar and met Alma, the General's daughter. The Croats were still besieging the east bank, still pounding it daily, and she had had to abandon her father's apartment and take shelter with another family. She still did not have word from her mother, but she met this journalist and asked him to carry a letter to me, written in her careful, schoolgirl hand.

Dear Janine: I am still here. We are all alive. Will you please telephone my cousins. Don't forget anything. Tell them everything you know about me. Alma.

There was no answer at the number she had given and when I went back to Mostar a few months later, she was gone. In the autumn, the General was transferred from Mostar to Sarajevo, I would sometimes see him at breakfast in the Holiday Inn, surrounded by his bodyguards. Once I had a drink with him in his son's apartment. We had woken the General from a nap, but he brought out a bottle of Loza and poured it into glasses while still in his slippers, saying '*Jivili*'. To Life.

Orhan and his father left Mostar and travelled overland, across the mountains to Sarajevo. Orhan was posted as a guard outside the Presidency. Some time later, he left Bosnia for Kuala Lumpur. I never knew why.

In Mostar, the dead were fading into history, in the same way that during World War II, during the fight for national liberation, one in ten of Mostar's inhabitants died, were buried in the cemetery and forgotten. Who remembered them, except for the very old? There was a cemetery with a monument in Mostar, but no one ever went there during the siege. There were no reminders left of those fighters, the ones that Tito described as the 'flower of [Mostar's] youth ... straight from their school benches they came, to take the places of the fallen, only to fall themselves fighting the occupying forces and the Quislings. They are the youth that not only Mostar but the whole of Yugoslavia can be proud of.'

The siege continued throughout the summer; and in November the Croats shot down Stari Most, claiming it was an important supply route for the Muslims. 'The bridge is not important to us,' a Croat commander told me one winter day in Medjugorje. 'Perhaps it meant something to the Muslims, but to us ... it was just a supply route.' There was no emotion, only bitterness in his shrug.

By early winter, there was a rope bridge in its place, over which the people, still besieged on the east bank, could run every morning to a pipe where they drained water from the Croats' supply. 'In their usual entrepreneurial way,' said Jerrie Hulme, the head of the UNHCR in Mostar, 'they have managed to survive.'

The town was levelled. Once, you could stand on the edge and look upstream and see the minarets and the arches of Koski Mehmed-Pasha mosque; or the fountain in front of another mosque. The Crooked Bridge was gone; Stari Most shattered; the tower of Halebinovka ruined. The old town and the bazaar were abandoned, except for gypsy families who were paid to run across the river to the west bank to find food. And the body count from 9 May 1993 to February 1994 was 1,360 people killed and 6,000 injured on the east bank alone.

In February 1994, nine months after the siege began, I went back to Mostar and stood in front of a building where three Italian journalists had been killed the week before: in the wrong place at the wrong time, bad luck. There were no roofs left in Mostar, there were now 57,000 people crammed into that space, but some of the people I knew were dead or gone. I made my way to the Armija headquarters. S. was gone, and Armand Bratonic, another commander I had known, whose family had let me sleep in their upstairs room, was so thin and gaunt, his cheeks hollowed out by nine months of starvation, that I walked past him on the street. His wife, Nadja, took me upstairs to show me the room where I had slept; it had been completely blown away by a shell; the back of it was open and the rain was pouring in through a hole in the ceiling.

'Your bed,' she said, pointing at a charred corner. And then she covered her mouth and laughed, because there was little else to do. 'Remember when you were here and we drank a beer?' And I had an image of Nadja, who was as thin and tiny as a child, drinking a beer that Philippe and I had brought from Medjugorje last summer. The look on her face had been one of complete joy. 'You brought a beer! And potatoes!' Now there was nothing left, not even my bed. Mostar, like a photographic image that had been left for too long in the developing fluid, was fading in time.

Amira the doctor was still in the hospital, still in the same basement room where I had sat with her nine months before, but she had had her baby and had gone back to work a few days later. Now the Spanish battalion was bringing her medical supplies, and the UNHCR had organised a mobile hospital out on the road leading to the old airport, but the beds were still full of amputees. The snipers on the other side of the river had not left their positions. Near the old town, the snipers were still out, targeting anyone who ran across the rope bridge to bring water back from the other side. One cold, rainy day, I wandered down near the river and found a gypsy standing by the ruins of the bridge. He shouted at me to get out of the way of the sniper, and then pulled his shirt up to show me a scar nearly two feet long running down his torso. He grinned – no teeth – and asked me for food, anything. His wife, Vilna, was pregnant and she lifted her blouse to show more scars: bullet holes stretched over her pregnant tummy. A younger sister sat in their hovel in silence.

On the other side of the river, on the west bank, the Croats were rebuilding their lives. On Rudarska Street the cafés were open, packed with burly HVO soldiers in Ray-Bans and greased-back hair, and the juice was served with ice cubes. There was traffic. For the first time in a year, petrol was available.

Some time later, in London, I read again my guidebook to Mostar. It was written in the early 1980s, published in Zagreb, badly translated. There is a section about Mostar's cultural and historical monuments and a photograph of Stari Most, and I stared at it, running my finger across the page, because I could still see the bridge with the tyres hanging over the edge and remembered Orhan laughing, drinking Loza, listening to U2 and singing, and Orhan saying, 'They'll never be able to kill our spirit . . . even if they have more guns.'

The guidebook came from another time, when Yugoslavia was still a country and neighbours weren't slaughtering each other, and it reminded me of something, of another image: once, in Sarajevo, I found a menu from 3 April 1992, a few days before the war began, when the hotel was still the headquarters of Radovan Karadzic's SDS party, before it was stormed by government forces, before there were snipers positioned on the seventh floor. On the menu, someone had left their breakfast order and had checked the boxes for room service the next morning, requesting eggs, orange juice, coffee, a newspaper. I remember when I found that menu how startled I was, because it seemed so long ago that anyone could get eggs or a newspaper in Sarajevo.

The same was true of Stari Most. I had never seen it except in war, first shelled, damaged but standing, with tyres hung around the walls to protect it, later, destroyed completely. I knew, because an old woman who gave me some withered cherries down by the river, told me it had survived thirty earthquakes. The guidebook says that from the beginning of its existence, Mostar has been a mixture of Eastern and Western culture and art, of the Continental and the Adriatic maritime cultures. Venetians, Turks and Austrians have come and gone, destroying and building. It says, ironically, that every historical period has left its mark.

TIME STOPPED

SUMMER 1993

THE POET STEVIE SMITH wrote about the futility of life in her poem, 'Not Waving But Drowning'.

> I was much too far out all my life,
> And not waving but drowning,

In Sarajevo that summer, there was a sense of drowning on dry land, or waving desperately and having no one see the appeal. It was tedious and hot, dry and tense with an ominous kind of anticipation, as though at any moment it could erupt into violence or anarchy. For days there would be minimal shelling, and then, when people felt safe and would go into the streets or to the market, the Serbs would send a mortar into a crowd as a reminder that they were still there in the hills. Driving up to their positions, the soldiers waved us down, motioned for cigarettes, crudely pointing at their open mouths. They would lead us into the dugouts, show us their guns proudly, then point to Sarajevo.

'Sarajevo,' they would say. 'All for Serbia.'

They made me sick, even if they were ignorant and stupid; I still think they knew what they were doing. But we stood and talked to them, gave them cigarettes. I am not sure why.

It was hot most days that summer; and still the Bosnian soldiers lay in trenches above the city, listening to Radio Zid and growing angry that below them, their friends were sitting in cafés. The defence of the city was vital that summer because the Serbs were pushing for the last of Sarajevo, trying to take Mount Igman, the strategic Bosnian supply route; to take Zuc, a hill behind the television centre. To permanently cut the city in half.

Sometimes, when the weather was good, it was easy to forget for a few minutes what was happening. One day, there was a football game in Dobrinja. A group of men took a deflated ball and began kicking it around in a parking lot, because the hills had been quiet for a few days they thought the snipers had gone into retreat. And then, perhaps because the weather was too beautiful, perhaps because the Sarajevans were not meant to be doing something so trivial as playing football during the war, a shell landed in the parking lot. When the crowd watching the game rushed in, trying to pull out the wounded and the dead, another shell landed, killing and injuring more. At the end of the afternoon they counted: eleven people were dead. When we arrived, the parking lot was covered in sticky pools of blood, in tendons, in muscles that had been ripped from limbs. The Dobrinja hospital was once again filled with the bodies of civilians who were maimed only because they wanted a game of football.

The next day, the UN launched an investigation to determine which side the shell had come from. 'It is not beyond imagining,' one UN source said, 'that the Bosnians would do this to their own side to get world attention. Remember, they are pushing for intervention. This might be something to trigger it.' But it wasn't, because as usual, no one gave a damn about so many people killed one afternoon in Sarajevo.

'Who would kill their own people?' asked Dr Zlatko Kravic, a doctor in Dobrinja hospital. He remembered the summer before when Dobrinja had been under siege for 52 days: a siege within a siege, so severe that the dead could not be brought into Sarajevo but were buried under the windows of apartment blocks. He used to operate with dentists' instruments. More than 6,000 people were treated in the hospital, on an operating table donated by General Morillon, surgeons digging into flesh without drugs for pieces of metal, for bullets.

Another afternoon, sitting at my bedroom window on a hot, lethargic Saturday, there is the whistle of a mortar, then the quiet aftermath, the delay before anyone realises what is happening, then the chaos, the panic. A shell had landed in the building directly behind the Holiday Inn, killing a family who were sitting on their balcony, thinking that maybe life was going to be normal again. I ran down the hallway to Dina, the BBC assistant producer whose parents lived near that building, and she was staring at her open window with a look of disbelief, beyond horror, beyond shock. 'Don't go down there,' she said. 'It's not worth it anymore.' We stood and stared, watching the crowd moving towards the site where the bomb fell as though it was happening in slow motion. People running towards the hole, the sound of screaming breaking the silence of the afternoon.

The Serbs targeted the places that were most important. There was a mortar that landed near a water queue: twelve dead, fifteen wounded, with more blood and bones, and the jerrycans still standing after the bodies were taken away. But that summer, everyone stopped counting the dead; we were all waiting for the last days on earth.

By midsummer, no one wanted to die for Bosnia anymore. The soldiers who had grabbed a Kalashnikov and run to the hills to defend their city were now cowering in cafés, anticipating the end of the war, and defeat. The commanders who had led brigades of untrained soldier lawyers, architects and students into the trenches sat in their headquarters with their heads in their hands, apologising to the families of the dead, counting their losses and mourning the betrayal of Aliya Izetbegovic, who was in Geneva, selling out Bosnia. The black-market cafés serving whisky pilfered from UN supplies were full of front-line soldiers who no longer wanted to take the last bullet for Bosnia.

Working in the television centre was Edin, a young soldier who had been a commander in Otes, one of the worst battles of Sarajevo, who had run away from home at the beginning of the war, begging to be taken to the front. One year later, he had lost his best friends and felt betrayed by politics and the government and so he was sitting inside with me one afternoon, smoking cigarettes, saying that he had had enough. He was lucky, he spoke good English and got a job working in television. 'No one wants to die anymore,' he said. 'We fought at the beginning, we put everything into it. Now, now, nothing is worth the bullet. We're not defending the city, we're not doing what we believed in. What is there left to believe in now?' He was eighteen years old.

All that summer, we waited for news of Mount Igman falling as the Serbs tightened their grip on the city. The aid convoys were frequently held up, and the West threatened air strikes again if the Serbs did not withdraw from their positions on Igman. By the end of July, another round of peace talks was set to begin in Geneva, but the Bosnian government threatened to boycott unless the bombardment of the city stopped. There was shelling in the city, sniping on the streets, in the water queues, near the river where children insisted on swimming, but the most intense fighting was on Igman.

You could see Igman from the airport road, looming, misty, green-shrouded, above the city. Across it, in the far distance, if you looked hard you could see a splash of white. It was a sheet, or a flag, but it was also a symbol. As long as it was stretched across the trees, it meant that Igman was safe, that Sarajevo would not be taken, that the people inside would be defended until the last soldier was killed on the mountain. It meant that Igman was also safe for supplies to come across in mule caravans, for food to reach the city when the convoys could not go, for arms to get across. To a city under siege, Igman was psychologically important. It meant that even if under siege, there was some way, however dangerous, to get out, or to get in. Without that route, Sarajevo was entirely encircled and if Igman, the Bosnian's last supply line, fell, it meant that the Serbs would take the city.

Since my first arrival in Sarajevo, the citizens' greatest fear was that Igman would fall, that the mountain which protected them from evil would be exposed to the enemy. And finally, in the summer, it became more than a fear, it was a reality: Didier François and Jean-Marie Le Maire, two French journalists, trekked to the top and came back reporting that the Serbs were mobilising, apparently getting ready for something. The Bosnians waited, and prepared their counter-offensive.

For weeks, we went to briefings and listened to the reports from Geneva and New York as the UN haggled over ceasefire lines, issued threats, drew the line in the sand, negotiated endlessly, threatened air strikes. Finally, in August, the UN marched 250 French troops up the mountain to make sure that General Ratko Mladic, the Serbian supreme commander, would march his men down. But Mladic was not easily convinced; even as the French troops mounted Igman and neighbouring Mount Bjelasnica, he was still playing for time. He knew he was winning. Even as the American F-16s flew overhead, Mladic would stand on his hillside position, binoculars pressed against his flaccid face. From Igman he could see all of Sarajevo, the final prize.

And what did Mladic actually see that August day when he looked down onto the city? Children, no longer concerned with snipers, playing in the Miljacka River, civilians still glancing over their shoulders as they ran past gaps between buildings. The ruins of the National Library, of the Institute of Oriental Studies, the shreds of the Parliament building, the yellow and brown stump of the Holiday Inn. An entire city of 300,000 people under siege, at the mercy of his whim as to whether or not the next aid convoy, the next Hercules loaded with rice, would get into the city. It must have felt stupendous; to think that despite everything, despite sanctions against Serbia, despite the disapproval of the West, he had a city in his hand. He could do whatever he wanted; no one was going to stop him. To prove the point, he continued to fly his helicopter to front-line positions on Igman, despite the fact that NATO had imposed a no-fly zone.

Finally, he was ordered to bring his men down, but they moved slowly, grudgingly. By mid-August, the Serb troops were in the last stages of their withdrawal from the hilltops, succumbing to diplomatic pressure after weeks of broken promises. From Trnovo, a ghost town south of Igman, 20 kilometres from the front line, they retreated in four buses, surly, vulgar, unshaven. 'We have not lost Igman,' one called out from his bus. 'We have won the war.' They stared at our small group of journalists with hostility and aggression. 'Fuck your mother,' one shouted to me as I sat on a kerb. 'Fuck you.' They still wanted to fight but the UN was forcing them off the mountain.

'It's a Serbian mountain,' Ratko, a 21-year-old, told me, glaring. 'It's a Serbian airport. The Muslims' (he spat out the word), 'are lucky that we let the West fly aid in to them. Ha! They should starve for another winter and then see if they can still fight with their old guns!'

Trnovo had been destroyed, the Orthodox church levelled, and the Bosnian Serb authorities who had taken us there walked through the ruins, picking up mortar cases and splintered furniture. 'The Muslims did this,' said Brncko, who worked in the press office in Pale. 'You always say we destroyed Sarajevo, but look what they did to us.'

'The Serbs took flak because we had bigger guns,' added a young English-speaking Bosnian Serb who called himself chief of staff. 'This was all painted as a war of Serbian aggression, but in fact, you can see for yourself that these were only local people fighting for their lives and their homes. They are not from Belgrade. They are from these villages, and the battle of Igman was a fight to defend their villages.'

The new Bosnian chief of staff was in his late twenties, had been educated in England, and had returned to assist in the war against the Bosnians, or as he called it, the 'Islamic war'. He fingered his new tweed jacket, bought in London, as he pontificated.

'You have to understand these people. The Serbs never wanted the war. It was imposed on us. We did not want to live as an Islamic country in the middle of Europe. We did not want our children to read the Koran and go to the mosque.'

Every day, the Serbs trickled down the mountain, but no one could tell us how many positions were still in place. They argued that the moment they pulled off the mountain, the Bosnian troops would advance and take their positions, an unrealistic assumption since the Bosnians were also being marched off the mountain. In August, the French soldiers brought me with Ariane Quentier and Didier François to the top of Igman. We stood at a windy point near the burnt television transmitter, and looked out in the direction of Sarajevo, onto the Brdo Valley where all we could see were columns of smoke: the Serbs burning positions as they pulled out. The plateau was littered with the remnants of battle: tins of food, trenches dug into the earth, bits of charred blanket, cigarette ends. Further down the mountain, the Bosnians were pulling out, leaving their positions, and there were bloody stretchers made from twigs left behind, tins of food, bits of paper, bloody field dressings. More than one year on top of this mountain, and now they were turning back, giving up.

The Serbs came after the Bosnians left, following their retreat. They burned all the Bosnian positions, burned them to the ground, there was a hotel in flames and the smell of incinerated wood. There was still the sound of mortars on the hill and a cemetery filled with bodies, soldiers on the mountainside who would never go back to their city. Some of the graves had no name, no date, just the place of death, maybe the regiment. On the way down the hill, there were dead bodies left in the trenches, unburied.

Ziam Zekovic, a commander in the Bosnian Army, a lawyer in his former life, was constantly in a state of despair. He was the deputy to the commander overseeing Zuc, the battle that was raging in the north part of the city, and every day, there were parents coming to him with tears rolling down their cheeks and he had to say things like, 'It's for Bosnia.' But even he didn't believe it anymore: on Zuc, in the trenches, the Bosnian soldiers were so close to the Serbs that you could see their flags waving barely fifty feet away. But they didn't have enough guns, enough food, or even cigarettes. Worse, they could hear the soldiers who had already given up the war talking, laughing, drinking in the cafés downtown. Zuc was strategic, but the battle of Igman was also strategic and the supplies of Bosnian fighters, those left who were not exhausted or wounded, were being depleted. 'They're trying to weaken us by shelling Zuc and making us fight there, taking men and arms off Igman,' said Cile, one of the Zuc commanders. 'In the past fifteen months, we've done wonders in Igman, but in my opinion, the Serbs want Igman and Stup and possibly the airport, and I doubt they will wait until winter.'

He estimated that there were about 2,300 Serbs on Igman launching tank and infantry attacks. In Stup to the east, and Hadzici, they were bringing in more tanks, closing in around the city, not to enter it, but to divide it.

The road to Zuc was littered with the shells of houses. It was a Sunday morning, another ceasefire had started at 10 am, the skies were clear blue, it was hot. We were sitting in a trench, helmets and flak jackets on, talking to soldiers about nothing: music, the beach, skiing. At 10.15, as we crouched, careful not to lift our heads higher than the top of the trench, the shells began to come in, so close that Cile shouted. Get out, and came and grabbed me by the shoulder, dragging me by the hand down the hill to where Ariane Quentier's car was parked. As we ran down the hill, we could smell the smoke, hear the whistle, then thud as the shell buried into the earth. The soldiers we had left behind with a few packs of cigarettes and some chocolates were fighting back with old rifles, maybe some were dead already, or dying. I fell once. Ahead of me Chris Helgren of Reuters dropped his camera and I stumbled over it. We jumped in the car and drove; Ariane pulled out muttering that the next time she would park facing out. A shell landed, close, as we skidded through the deserted streets, going down the mountain and back into the city.

It was a Sunday. I didn't have a deadline; even if I had witnessed something amazing I could not file because my paper did not go to press for a week. I got back to the Holiday Inn covered in mud, stones in my shoes, in my helmet. My hair was matted with sweat and dirt. At the Armija headquarters, checking in with Zaim to say I was alright, I was told that seven soldiers had died, according to his latest report. He led us into his office and lit a cigarette. 'Sarajevo is going to survive. The important thing is that Bosnia has survived because of Sarajevo.' He didn't sound like he believed it. We had some whisky, even though it was morning, and then I went back to the hotel because he was sending more reinforcements to Zuc.

What I remember most about the end of July is lying in bed listening to the fighting near Zuc and thinking of those soldiers

and how young most of them seemed. I started keeping track of
the shells coming into the city:

> 27 July 1993: Infantry attack on Zuc hill. Heavy shelling.
> 2,000 shells into Zuc and lip of Sarajevo. Seven rounds at TV
> centre; rounds fired near French Battalion 4, within 400
> metres. The UN says (ludicrously) it's not an attack on a
> position and they 'suspect' Serb artillery. They gave us typhoid
> pills to put in the water at the hotel today. Barry Frewer
> (UNPROFOR spokesman) told a newly-arrived journalist
> who asked a question this morning: Welcome, this is the kind
> of madness we have all been facing . . .

Down the hill from Zuc, Sarajevo was being torn apart by a war
within. Betrayed by politicians, by their own government, by
the West, the inevitable happened; the mafia who had always
lingered on the sidelines in Sarajevo began to tear it apart.
Territory within the city was beginning to be etched out like a
map within a map. Warlords sprang up, suddenly you could not
go to a certain part of town because it was controlled by Caco,
an infamous warlord, or his men from the 10th Mountain
Brigade. In July, a French officer from the Skenderija battalion
on good terms with Caco brought myself and Ariane Quentier
for a meeting with him. He sat in an overstuffed chair, with the
green crescent, the Islamic symbol, on the wall behind him. He
told us a crude joke which I did not understand about Lord
Owen, homosexuals and maps of Bosnia. Then he talked about
his men on the loose in Sarajevo, finding civilians in cafés and
pulling them into the trenches to dig.

'My men are in the trenches, fighting for the city,' he said,
gulping orange juice made from humanitarian aid packets. 'And
they are sitting eating beefsteak in cafés. Yes, I come and take
them away. The Bosnian Army is completely useless.'

The Armija, in turn, was splitting into factions, and its alliance with the HVO in Sarajevo was also falling apart. 'It seems to me that this is the worst situation since the beginning of the war,' said Slavko Zelic, the commander of Sarajevo's HVO, a thoughtful man who had once run a chemical company. 'A lot of the fighters are being sent out of Sarajevo to fight in Central Bosnia, we don't have many men left, and this is the longest we have been without electricity.'

The small band of HVO fighters in town was being attacked by the Armija. In the trenches across from the Holiday Inn, behind the Parliament building, the HVO soldiers complained that they were taking rounds from the Bosnians. A few months later, Zelic was thrown into prison; when I tried to get word to him, I was told he had gone to join his wife in Split. 'This is a crazy war,' he used to say. 'Madness and insanity.' It had taken on a new dimension of madness.

Caco and the gangsters grew more influential, and began to impose a curfew of fear throughout the town: there were weeks when the streets of the old town were out of bounds: no one wanted to venture into districts where his men were operating, television crews were losing money, their flak jackets, their armoured cars to soldiers with guns sent by Caco.

Two months later, travelling with a Canadian TV crew, I was stopped by Caco's men. Despite the fact that we were being taken by a prominent Bosnian commander from the old town to the trenches near Trebevic, and that I had already met Caco, they marched us at gunpoint into their subterranean headquarters and took our flak jackets. 'For the cause,' one said, ripping it off my shoulders.

'You bastards,' one of the crew mumbled. 'We risked our lives to report on your war.'

They didn't listen, or care. The commander we were with argued that we were journalists going to the front. They shouted back, angry, and took the jackets.

One month later, Caco was killed – an inside job, someone in Sarajevo, not a Serb.

★

Blackie and I are sitting in a café. Blackie's drinking whisky and I'm drinking a coke that cost 20 DM and he's telling me about his nightmares: every night, he sees the faces of the eight men he killed when he was a sniper on the Bosnian side. He's a Serb, but he was born in Sarajevo. 'One was blond . . . ' He ticks him off on his finger. 'And one was dark and one was, Oh God, I'm sure it was a guy I went to school with. That's the worst when you're a sniper, you see their faces because you target them for hours.'

The worst nightmare is one that really happened. He became a sniper because one day in April 1992, he saw a young woman, beautiful, with short black hair, red shoes and a red bag shot by a sniper in front of him. He stood with a group of people and watched her writhe in agony. He tried to reach her but no one could pull out her body because every time they tried, the bastards on the hill kept on shooting her, but not to kill: in the leg, in the breast, in the arm. Finally, she died and her body stayed there for three days. He kept seeing the red shoes, the bag, the short skirt. He could not get her face out of his mind.

So he goes to the police and becomes a defender of the city, in the special forces. Ten of them, elite commandos working behind Serb lines in Grbavica. You know what you do when you get a guy and you don't want to kill him? You think of that woman, that red bag, that short skirt. Then you slice their throats, or you pull the trigger. In July, he goes to Dobrinja, and he's on the sixth floor, in a sniper position, a gun nest with another soldier and they're getting hit with tank rounds from a Serb position in a church. For six hours, Blackie is crouching down, and he's praying, trying to remember his prayers and his two friends are blown away in front of him. 'We worked and lived together for 24 hours. We were closer than a family.' When they killed someone, they marked it down, in a diary. Blackie killed eight Serbs with a bullet to the head, maybe more.

He left the special forces after Stup. Now he's waiting, he doesn't know for what, but he feels like he's drowning all the time, like he can't pull his head above the water. He can't breathe, he feels the way Mario Susko did when he was buried under that wall after the mortar attack, but Blackie is not so much frightened as he is full of bitterness and hate. So much hate for the people who ruined his life that some days he can't get out of bed, can't get through the night without getting impossibly drunk, picking up two girls at a time, getting laid, not really caring who with.

'In those months after Stup,' he says, 'I was blinded with hatred.' This is Blackie, who before the war had a BMW, a small business and a wife with several diamond rings. 'All I wanted to do was kill, and kill and kill. Now, no one wants to die for Bosnia anymore. No one wants to take a meaningless bullet because at the end, who is going to remember you and what you did?'

So we wait, like sleepwalkers really, as Sarajevo begins to fall apart. We are depressed, there are days when I cannot write, even in my diary, because everything is the same.

The Serbs understand this psychology, the psychology of a city under siege ripping itself apart from within, spiralling into anarchy. Even so, everyone convinces themselves that if the Serbs overrun Igman, and effectively take Sarajevo, they will never enter it. The Bosnians have no arms, but they have more men than the Serbs. There is still a kind of terror that the end is coming any day. There is a fear that is even greater than the loss of innocence, of purity: a fear that everything, all the fighting, all the loss, has been for nothing.

And if the Serbs enter the city, what will happen? Will they torch it the way they did Jajce, or level it like Vukovar? The Bosnians reassure us: the Serbs are afraid of frontal attacks. It is easier to be a coward with a gun: to sit on the hills and launch mortars, than to enter a town and fight hand-to-hand battles. And the Serbs also realise the inevitable: that once they destroy Sarajevo with their guns, the people inside will have become so weary, so accustomed to violence and mayhem, that they will begin to tear apart the bits that are left themselves. They wouldn't have to risk their lives by entering the city; they could leave it to the Sarajevans to destroy themselves.

They waited. Across the front line in the *Republika Srpska*, twenty minutes by car in the old days, one hour if you were lucky now, the Bosnian Serb government was not content with the fact that they had practically destroyed Sarajevo. They wanted to humiliate it. I remember something a soldier told me once, that during World War II, the thing that infuriated the Germans more than anything during the siege of Leningrad was the fact that while they hovered outside, despite the hunger, the dead, the fighting, sometimes they could hear the people inside making music. And it drove them mad that they were unable to destroy that spirit, even if they could rip the city to pieces.

Once a week, we drove across the airport road to Pale, capital of the *Republika Srpska*, to buy petrol (rather than pay 30 DM a litre on the black market in Sarajevo), tomatoes and watermelons from the farmers who piled their fruit and vegetables on tables by the side of the road. It was difficult to buy things, because you had to bring something back for everyone: eggs for Vesna, tomatoes for Zoran, thick jars of plum jam, containers of orange juice, bars of chocolate.

Entering Pale was even more surreal than entering Sarajevo for the first time because this was a mountain village less than 20 kilometres south of Sarajevo, where people now being destroyed used to come on weekends to ski. The old bus stop opposite the Holiday Inn used to be packed every Saturday morning with crowds of people with skis over their shoulders, waiting for the short trip up the mountains, past the roads that are now dug in with trenches and hung with signs outside the soldiers' huts: CHETNIK CAFÉ, and through the pine trees, the woods, down the hill into Pale.

Now Pale was grim, even though you could buy fresh fruit and vegetables, even though you could get a hot shower at the Hotel Olympic, even though there was meat that did not come from a humanitarian aid tin. The people looked well fed, but suspicious; they did not like outsiders because the world was against the Bosnian Serbs, and they were reluctant to talk, to share, to communicate. Once, when I visited a Serb family from Sarajevo with close relatives still inside the city, the husband and wife looked at me with a kind of horror and asked me, please to be careful when leaving because the neighbours knew that a journalist had been there, and that I had come from Sarajevo. 'They hate us,' the woman said. 'Even though we are Serbs, we are Serbs from Sarajevo. We lived with Muslims and so we are tainted by them.'

The government offices were full of the same paranoia. I had spent many late nights drinking with Todor Duttina, the French-speaking poet turned Minister of Information, throughout the winter, when he would lecture us on the impossibility of co-existence. Now, in the summer, he sat with me over a steaming dish of fatty meat which I felt too sick to eat, cabbage salad and glasses of the sweet powdered orange soda that passed as juice. 'Drink some brandy,' he urged, but I could not touch the slivovitz that he was pushing. He stared at me.

'You know, every time I see you, you look older and angrier,' he said calmly.

I said nothing, pushing the meat about my plate.

'No, I mean it. What are you doing here? Why? Why don't you go home and have children now. The war is over. You know who won. Tell me why you stay.'

I dropped my fork. It seemed pointless to explain to him a commitment that anyone felt towards Sarajevo. 'Because the war is not over. Too much has been lost.'

'And because you think you have a vision of Sarajevo?' he scoffed. 'The dream that all of you had that Sarajevo was multi-cultural, multi-ethnic no longer exists,' he said, cutting his meat daintily into pieces. 'We do not want to live together anymore.' He chewed, and then spoke with his mouth full: 'Let me ask you, bluntly. If a man forces you to sleep with him, do you ask him to live with you afterwards? Who could possibly think we can co-exist after this war. Do you still believe in Sarajevo?'

I stared at him because there was nothing to say; he was right, how could these people ever live together again? How could one believe in a city that was losing all sign of life? Todor smiled and replied in French, 'You are a necrophiliac. How can you believe, how can you love a city that is dead?'

We drank coffee and he had plum brandy and then I shook Todor's hand and kissed his cheek and drove across the airport, twenty kilometres back to Sarajevo. It had been a terrible morning of shelling, 680 impacts by midday, 3,777 rounds from Serbian positions onto the city. I had only been away for a few hours but the smell of explosives was the first thing I noticed as we drove down Snipers' Alley, parked the car in the back of the Holiday Inn and ran into the back door. Inside, there was the dull shock, here we go again, and the hospitals were full, the stretchers bloodied with the 49 wounded and the seven dead, and I could hear Todor saying: 'You are a necrophiliac, how can you love a city that is dead?' He had known, even while we were sitting having lunch, that General Mladic, or someone, had given orders to shell the city and that while we were eating and drinking, someone was dying, losing a limb, getting shrapnel through the heart.

Towards dusk, when the sun went down, the cafés were full, places selling a cup of coffee for 10 DM, a pizza for 50 DM and a glass of whisky for 20. Off Marsala Tito Street, I was drinking a glass with a friend and at the next table a soldier was exchanging a bag of hashish with a comrade who pulled a bottle of Johnnie Walker Red from his backpack. At the next table a man in uniform was smoking Marlboros – inconceivable in Sarajevo, available only to journalists – and listening to a Walkman. Where had he got batteries and Marlboros in a city under siege for eighteen months? My friend, a former soldier who now peddled goods on the black market ('What can we do? It's a war'), ordered another whisky at the bar.

'What's happened to this place?' I said.

'Oh, it's easy, really easy,' he said. 'One day all of us woke up and realised that everything we believed in was wrong. Because the Bosnia that we wanted can never exist again.'

General Francis Briquemont, a senior UN soldier, called a press conference in the Delegates' Club the next morning. The fighting was continuing on Igman. Zuc was in danger of falling. There was pressure on Sarajevo. 'It is a confused atmosphere,' he said, all but throwing up his hands. 'And an atmosphere of distrust.'

Amidst the confusion, the city settled into lethargy, and a struggle began between the people who still believed there was something to win, who still believed in fighting for the Republic of Bosnia, and those who did not, who were too tired of the fighting and the blood and the misery. There was a lot of drinking that summer, a lot of drugs, a lot of black-market exchanges, a lot of sex, a lot of lying, deceit, maybe as a way of forgetting. There were women, mothers with children, who found their last bit of lipstick and put on their last lacy bra left from before the war, and walked down to Skenderija to try to sell themselves to the soldiers for some food, some Deutschmarks, a carton of cigarettes. 'It seems to me,' said one French soldier, a friend who would sometimes come at night and talk to us in our office on the fifth floor, talk about his rage and frustration, unable to fire back at the Serbs, even when they defiantly targeted UN positions, 'that we are headed for a breakdown.'

But by the end of July, all the cafés and restaurants had been closed. The Bunker, the putrid disco that had opened on the front line, where vodka sold for 7 DM and local cigarettes for 10, was boarded up. 'It is not fair for the soldiers on the front line to be fighting when the gangsters are sitting in cafés,' was the official response from the Armija. Caco, before his death, roamed the city in his truck, taking men who were not in uniform and dragging them to the front. My friends went undercover; Sead, the waiter who used to play football in the abandoned dining room at the Holiday Inn, was carted off one morning on his way to work and everyone was afraid of something, of a kind of anarchy, a darkness that was descending over the city. Susan Sontag arrived in town to stage *Waiting for Godot*; but, as one of the actors told me later, bumming a pack of cigarettes from me, 'We are really waiting for the barbarians.'

I found a bottle of whisky in Split one weekend and brought it back for Zaim, who was locked inside his headquarters. His dog had run away, he was gloomy. 'She's gone again,' he said, as though he was talking about a woman. 'Usually she comes back after a day. Now it's been three.' Five minutes earlier, as I entered his office, he had motioned me with his hand to wait: then a man and a woman emerged, crying, the woman's hand covering her mouth, her face twisted with grief. Zaim was walking next to them, with a look of bleak resolve on his face, and a terrible look of guilt, as though to say, forgive me. They looked at me, leaning against the wall, and I knew without being told that their son had been killed on Zuc the night before. 'I'm sorry,' I said. It sounded weak and careless, unemotional. The mother stared ahead.

When they left, Zaim motioned me inside and sent for coffee. We shared cigarettes and said nothing. A few days before he had given me a gift, a fountain pen, and he nodded when he saw I was using it. Then his face fell again.

'I hate everything about this,' he said. 'Everything. Do you believe in safe havens? To me, it means we are living on something like an Indian reservation.'

If in May, during the first air-strike threats, there had been a sign of hope in Sarajevo, all of the hope was quickly evaporating. The city had been declared a safe haven by the United Nations, but the shelling continued. At the end of July, the Serbs defiantly peppered Zetra, the French battalion's tank positions with 68 rounds in 45 minutes. General Briquemont called for 2,000 more troops and said, 'Sarajevo in the future has not to be a zoo.'

Inside the zoo, some people were trying to live, to grow up, to be as normal as possible, to fall in love. In the middle of the air-strike fever and of the retreat from Igman, I met Miss Sarajevo. I first noticed her in the dining room of the Holiday Inn one morning, surrounded by photographers: she was blonde, tall, with liquid green eyes. She was beautiful but hard: she wore tight Levis, a low-cut red blouse, red fingernail polish, carefully outlined red lips. She had dyed her short hair so that the dark roots were clearly visible. She was seventeen years old and looked thirty; there were faint, small, spider-like lines around her eyes and her mouth. Her name was Inela Nogic, she was introduced to me by a friend as 'the most beautiful girl in Sarajevo'. She blushed when we shook hands: her red nails were like talons.

She invited me to her apartment in Ali Pasino Polje, where corn was growing from balconies and the shelled brown buildings were used for barricades, and where everyone walking had a jerrycan filled with water. 'She's still my little girl,' said her mother Izeta, ruffling her hair, but Miss Sarajevo looked sulky, angry. She said she felt empty. 'So tired of everything, but even too tired to express my feelings.' She shrugged and took me to an illegal café, Café Clown, which was hidden from the street by blackout curtains. She sipped coffee, added two teaspoons of sugar (where had it come from?), played with her long nails, picking at the cuticles, and looked bored.

'Becoming Miss Sarajevo,' she said, referring to the beauty contest the week before, in which girls had walked across the stage in swimming costumes carrying banners that said 'Don't let them kill us', 'means that all this monotonous boring life has been changed and something new has appeared.' Then she sighed deeply and turned her attention to her hair, which she told me she dyed with washing bleach because she was bored one afternoon and there was shelling so she could not go outside. 'But immediately afterwards, everything became the same. I can't leave Sarajevo and compete in international contests. I can't become a model.'

Miss Sarajevo used to lie in bed when she was a small girl, dreaming of becoming a model, an actress, someone famous. She was beautiful, at her peak, and stuck inside Sarajevo with all of these dead bodies that couldn't even be brought to the cemeteries. 'They are dead, and I'm alive, but I'm dying slowly.

'And now my best years can't be used,' she said. 'These are the most important years. Can you understand? Can you? No you can't.'

Her boyfriend Boris, the first love of her life, was on the other side. He was a Serb. Before the war, when she was at the technical high school, and he lived in Grbavica, then a fifteen-minute walk from her house, now occupied by Serbs, they used to go sit in cafés, get drunk, hold hands. 'Most of my friends are dead now,' she said in a flat voice. 'Or on the front line.'

Miss Sarajevo reads the same fashion magazines, the old ones from before the war, over and over again. I say I have a two-month-old copy of *Vogue* back at the hotel and her eyes widen. She shows me some of her clothes; plaid leggings, midriff-baring cotton tops from summers when she would sit outside in cafés all day. Now she trades clothes with her girlfriends and says she 'gets used to everything'.

But the most important thing in her life at this moment, in the summer of 1993 in Sarajevo during her eighteenth year, is her makeup, which she lovingly saves and stores in the bedroom littered with posters and English words like 'Kiss My Ass' and old records. There's a doll on the floor, and a bottle of Givenchy perfume that a journalist gave her, an old compact filled with sticky powder, a lipstick almost gone, a bar of soap cut in half. 'It's my own form of resistance,' she says, to wake up every day, try to find some water, wash her short hair and spend fifteen minutes making up her face with the last bit of lipstick that she has kept from before the war.

She wakes up every day at 10 am and stays in bed until 2 pm, because she is bored and there is nothing else. She might read a book, Harold Robbins, or play cards. If the shelling isn't too bad, she might sit in the sun, playing her guitar, or if there is enough water, throw a bucket over her head, pretend she is at the sea. She thinks about the last night she was with her boyfriend, in April the year before, getting drunk on *pivo* in a café. She says she's lost something, she doesn't know how or what, because she had to survive, like everybody. 'I have to be serious now,' she says. 'But I still laugh. What can I do? I can't cry.'

She wants to be Linda Evangelista. And at night, after she plays Deep Purple or Rolling Stones songs on her guitar, she has dreams. There is one of her and her best friend Nina, who is a Serb and went to Belgrade at the beginning of the war. They are walking on the beach together. For a moment, they are fifteen again, and they are in love with their boyfriends, and there is no war. No one has died. The buildings around her house, where twenty shells fell five metres away from her door, are not destroyed. Nothing has happened. Time is not standing still, but moving ahead. There is no war.

★

Irma Hadzimuratovic was lying on a cot, her spine twisted awkwardly, on the fifth floor of the State Hospital in Sarajevo. Her tiny hands, with their fingernails painted red, were curled into mitts. Her eyes were opened but unfocused, her breathing was heavy, panting, like a dog.

I had run up the five flights in the dark, stumbling because I had forgotten my torch, to the intensive care unit where the five-year-old was being held, and where she had become, overnight, a *cause célèbre*. The press had been banned from the room, but I had come up the back way and when I reached her room, I was not alone: Irma was surrounded by three American network cameramen I had never seen in Sarajevo before, who were adjusting lights and wires near her bed and discussing the angle at which to take the shot. Irma lay unblinking, holding a dirty toy animal.

I don't know why I didn't feel anything as I looked at her, at the tiny painted fingernails that a friend of the family later told me were painted by her mother before the mortar attack. I thought, as I looked at her, that maybe I needed a break, needed to get out of Sarajevo because I didn't feel anything for her. She was another girl, another one who had been unlucky. Not waving but drowning.

The scene had been played so many times. When had I seen this before, that same face, the same grimace of pain, the doctor frustrated and angry, the American camera crew hopping around the bed, anticipating the splash on the six o'clock news?

Tuzla, four months earlier. The retreat from Srebrenica, the soldiers marching single file, most of them with stumps wrapped in gauze, balancing on one crutch. The open-backed trucks packed with refugees, many of them cleansed not once but twice from their villages in eastern Bosnia, that bizarre look of fear, anger and confusion on their faces. The hospital, the ward where thirteen-year-old Sead Bekric was lying, beneath a cartoon sketch of Donald Duck, his eyes bandaged, his freckled face cut and bruised, his hands reaching out across the sheet to touch mine, to feel my face, his damp hands tracing the outline of my mouth, his tears and confusion. Nearly all the bones of his face were broken and breathing hurt; his voice was raspy and exhausted.

'When can I take the bandages off?' he asked a nurse who came into the room with a painkilling injection. 'When will I be able to see again?' She flinched, embarrassed. 'Be patient,' she said to him, smoothing back his hair. The other eight men in the room, all wounded in the same mortar attack in Srebrenica, looked away helplessly. 'The people who did this cannot even be called people,' said one of the men tonelessly, playing cards by himself.

Sead did not remember much: a football match in Srebrenica, the promise of a celebration, with instruments, music. He had been living under siege, under attack for so long, had become used to hand-to-hand fighting, to rockets in the streets, to mortars, but because he had lived through the worst, he walked with his friend to the muddy field. Because it was sunny and it seemed as though maybe the spring was coming early in April, there were people out on the streets. At 2.15 pm, the intense barrage began.

When the two shells landed nearby in the schoolyard where Sead was playing, he fell to the ground unhurt. After a few minutes, he got up and rushed to the side of his friend, who was injured, tripping over bodies and pieces of dismembered limbs, hunks of flesh. He grabbed his friend's arm and pulled, began to tug him away from the blood and the bodies, not knowing where he would take him, anywhere but here, when the third shell landed. Sead fell again, and remembers that 'I felt like something fell on top of my head.' Seventeen children dead, seventeen children wounded, in one hour.

Louis Gentile, an aid worker in Srebrenica for the UNHCR, remembers watching the casualties coming in on anything that could be moved: wheelbarrows, ox-carts. 'It was more than injuries. There were bodies that were completely blown apart. There were people with what seemed to be their brains coming out of the eye sockets. I went to the schoolyard an hour after the first barrage. There were still seven bodies just lying there, two more children. One seemed to be about six years old, the same age as my son and he had no head left at all. Where the kids were playing football, there was a fenced-in area covered in human flesh. Even on Tuesday when I left with the convoy, there was still human flesh clinging to the fence where the kids had been playing football.'

Sead woke up on a stretcher, he remembers there was a bandage, a dirty one because he could smell it, over his eyes and his fingernails were encrusted with blood. He didn't remember the next part, lying on the stretcher crying in pain, then being loaded into the back of an open-ended truck, finally arriving in

Tuzla under the arc of television lights, being photographed with his hands clasped obediently behind his neck.

He remembered this: a village called Voljivice, a beautiful farm, a horse, a cow, a pig, some sheep. Riding the horse in the fields, in the winter, the walk to school with friends across the snow, the quietest village, the peace, the silence, the river. The summer swimming, then the autumn, then the winter, then the spring when the war began. Then, one morning walking into his classroom with his books under his arm and the teacher crying, saying that there would not be any school. Leaving his house, living in a forest with his parents, leaving the cows, the pigs, the sheep, the village. In May, walking to Srebrenica with his family, living off corn and cattle food, and finally MREs that came from the sky, when the Americans began to airdrop. Running outside and fighting with the other boys for the packages of food, then running inside when the shelling began because the Serbs usually waited for the moment when the crowds descended, like animals, to tear at the packages because they had not eaten for so long, drop in a shell or a round.

Sead lived with the war for so long that he no longer felt at risk. He knew that sometimes he should not go out, but he could not stay in a basement forever. The day of the football game, the sun was shining and he wanted to go. 'I wanted to play,' he said.

The impact of the shell that fell on the field had literally destroyed his eyes and broken the bones in his face so that they were pressing down against his nose, making breathing impossible. At night, he complained because of the pain behind his ears, and because of the fear and confusion: his mother and sister and his brother were staying in a refugee shelter 20 kilometres from Tuzla and when they could find a ride, they came and sat weeping by his bed, not answering his questions about his eyes.

His doctor in Tuzla, Ibrahim Pasic, said that he would never see again. He said that Sead did not know he was blind. 'Who are you?' Sead said, the small hands touching my face. 'Where is my mother?' He wanted to unwind the gauze, he told the nurse deliriously. 'I would give anything to know what has happened to my eyes.'

Later, talking to Pasic in his office over strong Turkish coffee, a story emerged: one of the British television producers, desperate to get a story, had asked the doctor if he would first tell the mother on camera, that her son was blind, and later tell the boy so that they could capture it on film.

'She told me it was important for the people of England to witness something like that,' he said, clearly shocked by the request but confused. Pasic said he did not want to tell Sead he was blind yet, because he wanted to give him hope.

But Sead, when I saw him later before his painkilling injection had taken effect, was not so sure. Even at the age of nine, he knew.

'When people ask me if I will go back to my village,' he said, grasping the sheet, 'I cannot even imagine it. I cannot imagine that I will ever live through this war.'

Those days in Tuzla, in March and April 1993, were the most emotional for me: seeing Sead and the amputees, the raped, the wounded, the abandoned schoolhouses full of refugees slowly going mad. And during the day, we would gather at an army headquarters, try to pick up the ham radio operator, the only link Srebrenica had with the world.

It took Sead Bekric and his shell-ravaged friends to send Margaret Thatcher into a rage. 'I am ashamed of the European Community, that this is happening in the heart of Europe and they have not done any more to stop it,' she said. 'It's within Europe's sphere of influence; it should be within Europe's sphere of conscience. There is no conscience. We have been a little like an accomplice to a massacre. We cannot carry on like that. Just imagine if our families were there, seventeen children killed yesterday, seventeen in an hour.'

In Tuzla in early spring, we waited, waking every morning to drive to the last Bosnian checkpoint before Srebrenica to wait for the truckloads of refugees, standing up, leaning against each other for support as they drove past us, staring, unable to believe that we were filming them, snapping pictures, asking these stupid questions, like, Where are you from? How was life inside Srebrenica? Doing nothing, because we knew that nothing was going to happen. They would be sent to centres, they would lose their homes, years of their lives. And it was only a matter of days, even hours, before the Bosnian Army retreated and Srebrenica fell.

For a few days, we hunched by the ham radio, believing for a few minutes that maybe something was going to happen because this little blind boy had triggered some reaction from the world. But nothing that had happened – not the hand-to-hand fighting, not the sight of the refugees, not the commander who came on the radio and pleaded, 'In the name of God, do something' could persuade the world to do anything. Malcolm Rifkind, the British Defence Secretary, dismissed Thatcher's outrage as 'emotional nonsense'. Lord Owen once again discussed the possibility of air strikes on Serb supply lines, but with scepticism. General Philippe Morillon, the UN commander in Bosnia who had brought Srebrenica's plight out into the open the winter before by breaking its year-long siege, contacted Serb leaders, pleading with them: 'For God's sake, control your commanders on the ground.' But they could not be controlled.

On Friday, 16 April, the Serb infantry had broken through the Bosnian front line southeast and northeast of the town. Fourteen international aid workers were trapped in town with the 30,000 terrified civilians. On the ham radio, a Bosnian soldier told us, 'Tell the world that we will not surrender. That we will fight to the end.'

On Saturday, 17 April, I sat up with the radio operators in Tuzla, monitoring the fighting in Srebrenica, chain-smoking, growing increasingly emotional as the voice came through, crackly and terrified, across the wire. 'The Serbs are getting closer ... We beg you to do something, whatever you can. In the name of God do something.' The radio operators in Tuzla were ashen-faced. The rest of us said nothing, just listened as the voice pleaded and begged us to get in touch with President Clinton, John Major, anyone. 'Does the world know about us?' it asked.

That night, there was hand-to-hand fighting in the town, and by the next morning, despite the fact that the UN Security Council had passed a resolution declaring Srebrenica a UN-monitored safe area and demanding the immediate withdrawal of Serb forces, it was clear that no one could impose that. A convoy of Canadian soldiers dispatched to Srebrenica to monitor the safe area turned back by Serbs.

The town was in agony. There were dead in the streets, 'like scenes from hell,' said the radio operator. The UN command post was hit by a mortar shell. The UN Security Council met again on Saturday night to consider tougher action, but nothing happened.

Srebrenica, a safe haven protected by the world, had effectively fallen to the Serbs.

With the Irma story in Sarajevo four months later, the press descended again. Overnight, as soon as the BBC broke the story, the airport was flooded with the popular press, photographers and television crews from all over the world, who had never set foot in the city before, did not understand the issues, the politics or the people and only wanted to find another Irma. They were only staying three or four days, they said, so they had to move quickly and they raced through the Holiday Inn with their flak jackets and their helmets bumping against their legs, bounding in and out of armoured cars, flashing Deutschmarks, looking both confused and hungry, and most of all insensitive.

'I am so sick of them,' said one of the more acerbic Bosnian journalists at breakfast one morning as she bit into a hard bread roll. 'They come here like vultures, looking for the dead.' She reported a story: that morning at breakfast, one of the reporters had gone up to her asking if she thought there would be a mortar attack that afternoon so that he could interview the victims. She smiled sardonically. 'The dead make very good copy, I'm beginning to see.'

But the doctor who was standing beside Irma's bed that afternoon was not smiling. She was tall with a mass of dark curly hair, a thin, sculpted face and dark brown, almost black eyes. Her arms were crossed in front of her chest and she was angry. She shouted at a nurse standing next to her in Bosnian to clear the press while the cameraman tried to argue that he was part of a pool and would share his pictures with the rest of the crews.

'I don't care!' the doctor spat in French. Then she turned to me.

'What are you looking at?' she said, and then softened slightly. 'How long have you been here? One day? Do any of you understand what is happening to this city, to this country?'

'Since the end of last September,' I said.

She stopped. 'Were you here in the winter?' I nodded and she motioned me into the side room and asked me for a cigarette. Her hands were shaking and; up close, I could see the purple circles of exhaustion under her eyes. She had been up for three nights in a row, and for two weeks she had been fighting with the United Nations to get Irma evacuated. She was bitter that it had taken the flood of press to embarrass them into action. She was sickened by the hypocrisy. She dropped her head into her hands and began to cry.

Vesna Cegnic was 36 years old, an anaesthesiologist, who had trained in Belgrade and who, in the days before the war, lived in an apartment in Grbavica, which she had abandoned at the beginning of the war, leaving everything behind but a few books and photographs that she took with her. She moved herself, her mother, and her younger brother Nino, a gifted architect, to a small apartment in Marijin Dvor, near the river, where they spent most of their time in the small kitchen. The front room, which faced the river and the snipers, was piled with sandbags. When there was gas, the kitchen was lit by a small amount that was pumped through medical tubing, and extracted with clamps from the hospital. For months, there had been no electricity; she was used to operating and administering anaesthetic by candlelight; she had become so accustomed to shells that her hand no longer shook when she was inserting needles into veins.

The first time Vesna saw Irma was only a few hours after the mortar attack. That was two weeks before the fiasco broke in mid-August. Irma's tiny body was twisted; her hands were clenched in bloody fists. As Vesna worked with the other doctors in the emergency ward, she heard the story: Irma's mother Elvira had thrown her body over her daughter's during the attack and had been ripped apart by pieces of flying metal. When a neighbour pulled the body off, Irma was crying, 'It hurts, it hurts.' It took time to find a car with petrol to take her to the hospital, fifteen minutes away, down Snipers' Alley. When they did, a neighbour held the tiny body on her lap and prayed, 'Please live, please live, please live.'

Irma's family were refugees in the neighbourhood; they had already been burnt out of one house and the block of flats that they had found across from the Television Centre was not safe from shells. Children usually did not play outside on the dried-out grass, but that day in the beginning of August was sunny and hot. Leila Dolovac, Elvira's best friend, decided that she would risk it and walk to the market to try to find a loaf of bread for them if Elvira watched the children. Tarik, Leila's son, said he wanted to stay inside, but Irma wanted to go out. He lived, Irma was dying. One lives, one dies, the old Sarajevo equation.

Cegnic was in the hospital when Irma was brought in, she remembers that she had 'never seen a child so helpless and a child who certainly did not have a chance to live. I think it is the saddest case I have ever had.' A few hours after she arrived, she had a massive convulsion. She needed a brain scan, but the only equipment they had was a stethoscope.

She spoke in the beginning, incoherent words, sentences, things whispered to the nurses who would stand by her bed. One night, she said she felt like she had a 'doll inside my stomach. It hurts.' The next day, she fell into a coma.

That day, Cegnic and Dr Edo Jaganjac began their siege of the United Nations, pleading with them to evacuate Irma. Vesna would walk to the PTT building in the morning, begging to see someone who could do something to get Irma out of the city. UNPROFOR would tell her it was not in their hands, that the evacuation procedure was handled elsewhere. They told her to phone Geneva, knowing very well that Sarajevo had not had international phone lines for over a year. She would walk back to the hospital in tears. For four days, the two doctors shuttled between officials of UNPROFOR and UNHCR, who then directed them to the World Health Organisation and the United Nations Children's Fund. All of them expressed concern, none of them could do anything. Tony Land, head of the UNHCR in Sarajevo at that time, told them that 'all we can do is provide a package and get them to the airport. We do not have donor countries.'

In the hospital, Irma shifted her position. Her head was rotated at an unnatural angle, and her spine was twisted. She could move her hands and she held the stuffed toy in a tight grip. Her lips were chapped, bloody, she was not eating. When Cegnic changed the bandage covering the twelve-inch wound that sliced down her abdomen, she would blink but not cry. The only medication they had was antibiotics. At night, the doctor sat next to Irma, her bed lit by candlelight because she would be frightened of the dark.

One morning, when it was clear that the hospital could do nothing for the girl, and that she would die unless she left the city, Jaganjac walked the ten minutes from the hospital to the Holiday Inn, climbed three flights of stairs to find Dina and Alan Little in the BBC office. When Alan broke the story later, concentrating on the UN's impotence and lack of cooperation, the press began to flood the city, but Sir Donald Acheson, Britain's Chief Medical Officer, now a WHO advisor, who was in town to discuss the crisis of the impending winter, refused to take our calls regarding the case and left town on Monday, aware that a major crisis was at hand.

Eventually, six days later, evacuation was arranged in a blizzard of press coverage, but Jaganjac was bitter as he stood behind a glass door watching French soldiers strap Irma onto a stretcher: 'It's too late,' he said. 'You see how quickly they can act when they want to? She needed to be evacuated a week ago, now it is too late.'

Cegnic did not sleep all that week. Every time she thought of the case, she felt anger rising that she could not control. 'We tried to help save a little girl, not only for her, but to change a system in the future. We don't want to evacuate a child without a chance. We want people to live. With Irma, it was a question of minutes and too much time was wasted.'

That night, I brought her some cigarettes. She was still angry, and kept walking by Irma's empty bed. When I said that Irma was going to Britain, she waved her hand to silence me. 'She's gone to England. So, I am angry because it is a political gesture. It's theatre.' She coughed and stared out the window of the hospital, towards the river, and past that, to the Jewish cemetery where the Serb artillery positions were dug in.

'I am not an actor and this is a life. This is not the beginning of the war. Where were all these people last summer?'

'But she's out, she's going to be alright now. At least one is out.'

She stared at me hard. She said, okay, now we will never discuss this issue again, this is the last time we are going to talk about it as journalist and doctor, but I will say it now and that is it. And she never did again, throughout the following months, when we would sit and laugh and share food and cigarettes, we never talked about Irma. Except when I would first get back to Sarajevo, when she would ask, 'How is she? Has she moved?'

That night, the night that Irma was taken out of the city, we sat in the hospital waiting room. There was a chocolate bar, half eaten, on the table, a packet of matches from an MRE, a torch that I had given to Vesna. She picked it up and played with it.

'I don't believe in God, but there is something up there in space and I am sure there is justice. Every person in the world must imagine what it would be like if this was their town, their family, their child. Then they will understand our agony. We need a miracle. This is not a war because war is front lines and soldiers. These are children. These are innocent people and this is not a movie. This is real life.'

When Irma flew out on the Hercules another batch of reporters, hundreds of them, were waiting for the tiny girl in Ancona. She was then raced to Britain where more waited at the Great Ormond Street Hospital. John Major turned it to his advantage, using her as a publicity coup. She is still there, her father is still there, her brother is still there, but she's no longer a *cause célèbre*. Last Christmas, she smiled and moved.

The summer ended in a kind of haze. A couple were killed on the bridge; they had just been married and were trying to escape across. Admira Ismic was Muslim and Bosko Brkic was Serb and they were killed by a sniper as they ran and no one could get to their bodies so they lay, entangled together for four days. Both sides fought over their bodies and they became another symbol of the war, Romeo and Juliet. The BBC ran it big that night, and the American papers, and later, PBS did an entire documentary on their family history, but everyone else inside was tired. They were just two more people dead.

That night, I was standing at my window with two other journalists working for ABC, Chuck and Shaney, and we were watching the sky for shooting stars. The entire city was blackened, scattered with the glow of a few candlelights, and so the stars had never been so prominent. From the hill, towards Zuc, came the sound of machine-gun fire, automatic weapons and the thud of mortar. Somewhere in the dark a radio was playing, and a song began, Pink Floyd, 'Wish You Were Here'. Then heavier machine-gun fire started up, drowning out the words, and I saw a shooting star.

'It's good luck, isn't it?' I said to Chuck, and he laughed.

'Not in this place,' Shaney answered.

THE BRIDGE

SHE COULD ALMOST SEE HIM from her kitchen window. One hundred metres from her, he is sitting in the living room of his flat, listening to the radio and sorting through his papers. He is moving slowly and painfully through the three rooms, opening the windows, letting air into the flat which stinks of cats and urine. His hands and feet are swollen and the clothes he is wearing are the same ones he has worn for weeks; he does not notice the smell, since his wife escaped across the airport two months ago, there are days when no one climbs the five flights and when he speaks to no one except the radio. He lives alone; today, he's wearing a woollen hat because it's bright but cold, and his brown felt slippers; he carries a wicker basket when he leaves the flat to collect wood.

Jasna, who is 42, saw her father, Muharem, for the last time the day the barricades went up: 6 April 1992. Then the walk from her flat to her parents' took about five minutes: along a small path, across the river, over the bridge called Brotherhood and Unity, and into Grbavica, a suburb that is now part of Greater Serbia. This is the place her father has stubbornly refused to leave even though he is a Muslim and most of his neighbours and friends, and all of his family were ethnically cleansed months ago. He was a partisan fighter with Tito during World War II, in Central Bosnia, which is where he met his wife, Nadja, and he is now old, but he still remembers his brigade and fighting in

148

the woods near Prozor. He was the commander of a small group of fighters then, he and Nadja married and their eldest daughter, Esreta, who is now fifty, was born in the woods. Then came Sabina, born in Sarajevo, then Jasna, then Naida, then Azra, then Sunita. They've all left Sarajevo now, except for Jasna, and the two of them are separated by a front line.

He is 78 but still tough: Serbs, he says, are not going to make him leave his home, even if the streets are burning and the flats are being used as sniper positions to target the bordering Muslim neighbourhood of Hrasno, where his daughter Jasna is now living. Serbs were always his neighbours. Why should they start hating each other now?

Grbavica has been held by the Serbs since the summer of 1992; when they entered the streets after fierce fighting, and the people who were left hung blackout curtains from the trees to protect them from the Bosnian snipers on the other side of the river. Muharem stayed after the curtains went up, in the block of flats gouged with shrapnel. One of his bedrooms was used as a Serbian sniper position, a gunner positioning his weapon out of his window to fire onto Sarajevo.

His memory is drifting: is it Sunita who is the doctor, or Naida? Which one is the psychology professor, which one is living in Belgrade, amongst Serbs? What day was it his wife said she could stand no more, crossed the icy river, then the bridge, and left the country for Moscow?

Muharem is not difficult to find in Grbavica, because there are not many Muslims left. A young Serb girl called Maya whom we met outside the supermarket takes me to his building near the river. She's only eighteen but looks so much older. Her mother was killed at the beginning of the war, then her father, and she is raising her sister Irma alone in a dismal flat.

'Who looks after you?'

'No one.' She says it quietly with a shrug of her shoulders.

'Sometimes the neighbours help, but it's my sister and me, and most of the time, we're all right.'

Maya has a kind of deep sadness. She asks about life on the 'other side' beyond Grbavica, and her shoulders are hunched over with a kind of guilt and apology that seem to say, I am a Serb, but a good one, and some of us are suffering as much as the people on the other side. She wears black since her mother, at 36 only four years older than me, was shot in the back running back to her flat carrying a string bag full of shopping. She was killed by a Bosnian on the other side of the river.

Maya is heavy with pale skin, dark straight hair and a full mouth. Her black clothes make her look much older; she says she will wear them for one year, in mourning for her mother, in the Orthodox tradition. The days when she lived on the other side and had Muslim and Croat friends seem in another lifetime. 'I don't believe in killing, I want my city back,' she says, but she knows, like everyone, that even if the Bridge of Brotherhood and Unity was opened up and people could move freely from one suburb to the next, find their families, begin again, it would never be the same. 'How could we ever live together again? Tell me that? Never, ever again, too much hatred, too much blood.'

Still, she leads me to the old man Muharem, because I have a letter from his daughter Jasna, one of his six daughters, whom I met on the other side of Sarajevo. Grbavica should be easy to get to, just across the bridge. But instead, the trip takes two hours or more, because you have to drive across the airport, cross the Serb front line, enter Serb territory and then take a back road that leads you into Serb Sarajevo. If you don't run into hostile soldiers, you can do it in just over an hour; if you're held at a checkpoint, or if you decide to go to the Lukavica barracks and formally ask permission to visit the *Republika Srfska*, of which Grbavica is a part, it can take hours and hours. But once you drive down the road, you're in another country: it's so strange to be driving down the hill and to see the Holiday Inn which is maybe 300 metres away, which you feel you could almost touch, but you know that it is in another country, another republic, separated by fear.

February 1994. There are 400 Russian United Nations troops in Grbavica now, with their APCs and heavy trucks, but there is tension in the city with their arrival. The Russians have been bonding with the Serbs, Slav brotherhood three fingers raised, and there is emotion as the Russians drive through the streets because the Serbs have always felt that they have been wronged in this war. And the Russians have been their allies throughout the war. The Russians are officially in Grbavica to monitor and collect the Serb heavy artillery, those weapons that were used to pound Sarajevo, and in the centre of town there are collection depots where the mortars and rockets and tin chests packed with ammunition wait to be taken somewhere else. In one regroupment area of Grbavica, boxes of Serb ammunition, mortars and heavy artillery are piled in a corner. And yet, not all the weapons are down from the hills: as in the retreat from Mount Igman in the summer of 1993, the Serbs stall, claiming they fear a Bosnian infantry assault.

Earlier that week two soldiers were killed in Sarajevo by Serb snipers, and the Serbs say it was the Bosnians who started it, the Bosnians who launched an assault on the Vrbanja bridge which separates their front lines. Now, it is the end of the week, and the UN is still lagging behind, saying that while most of the heavy artillery has been moved, not all weapons are yet under their effective control. The market, scene of the massacre three weeks ago in which 68 people were killed, has reopened and the streets are full, but there is still sniping from the riverfronts separating the city, and the aftermath of the market massacre has been bizarre: no one quite believes it has happened this late in the game, this kind of carnage still happening. People walk through the streets like sleepwalkers and the score is still not settled.

The Serb soldier guarding the weapons is blond and speaks good English, but he is resentful and surly. He's called Micho, he's an officer, and he keeps saying to me, 'I know you hate me, why are you so angry with me?'

'I'm not,' I say.

Micho says, kicking a piece of ice that covers the ground, 'My Muslim neighbour is not my enemy but the Muslim fighter is. We cannot speak of Brotherhood and Unity after two years of bloody war.' He gives the usual Serb line: before the war, he had Muslim brothers, friends, now they can never live together again. He doesn't believe all the propaganda against the Serbs, as for the bombardment and destruction of Sarajevo, a city he spent all of his life in, he says it was all done in self-defence.

'Self-defence,' I say, writing in my notebook and mentally making a note about the arms embargo. 'Against the Bosnians, who have barely enough weapons to defend the city?'

Maya nods.

'Sarajevo must be divided,' Micho adds, but he doesn't sound so sure.

We walk around the area. The people stare, openly hostile, and rush into buildings. Grbavica is strange: suspicious, grim, lacking any kind of spirit. Before the war, it was a community of 40,000, a few hundred metres from the centre of the city, but when the war started half of the inhabitants, mostly professionals, fled. Now it's occupied by Serbs who moved into the boarded-up apartments and can look down on Sarajevo from the hills, and see the city burning, can see the tall buildings in Hrsno, near Heroes' Square, on fire. A small group of Muslims, probably crazy, refused to leave. One of them is Muharem.

We run to get to his building – Jasna scribbled the address by candlelight on the back of my notebook – because Maya is frightened of snipers. It feels strange to be on the other side, and threatened by Bosnians, who might shoot me just because they think I'm a Serb, the same Bosnians who always said that they would never shoot at civilians. But now, just because I'm in the wrong territory, I am the enemy too, even though I've sat in their trenches and loaned them my helmet and gone up to give them cigarettes and cans of coke that cost 20 DM on the black market. Now, there is no sign that says I'm a journalist and even if there was, would it matter?

There's a madwoman outside Muharem's block of flats; she wants cigarettes but I have none. When I say *nema, nema*, none, she screams at me, a terrible guttural call. I flinch, because it sounds like a curse, and Maya motions with her head to keep moving. It's muddy and we climb over rubble but we enter the wrong building and Maya stops abruptly because there is a drawing of a human body with circle targets on it, like a dart board, and points for the head, the heart and the lungs: a snipers' practice target, littered with practice bullets. We stare for a minute, Maya takes my hand and we run outside, into the next building.

Inside Muharem's building, there is a sniper nest in the first apartment we enter and the soldiers sit up and grab their guns when we tentatively stick our heads around the corner. One leans over defensively and almost shields his face. 'Get the fuck out of here,' he shouts in Serbo-Croat. Maya blanches, moves back, frightened, but the other soldier who is younger and has a softer, fuller face stands and moves us out of the room quickly, and leads us to the third floor where every door is splintered and kicked in. The door to a flat in the corner is still intact and the solder bangs at it until an old man with a bewildered look opens it and squints at us. He sees the Serbian solder and his face drops as if to say: not again.

I hold out my hand and he stares. 'Jasna,' I say, and the soldier repeats it.

'She's got a message for you from Hrasno,' the soldier shouts, not unkindly, because the old man is slightly deaf. 'From your daughter.'

The old man's eyes widen slightly; he is confused. 'Jasna?'

Jasna is one of the six girls he raised, but when he leads me inside, he still cannot remember all their names. 'Jasna?'

We sit down and he opens the door of the kitchen, riddled with bullets. Aside from the kitchen, he lives in practically one room. It smells so bad that Maya covers her nose when he is not looking, but he insists on making us coffee, and tries to give us a kind of chocolate spread that he's kept in a jar. Then he leads us through the apartment: through the tiny kitchen to the room where he lives and sleeps with the radio blaring rock and roll, and his medals and the last of his Economics books. Another room is locked; it was the snipers' room.

He says he used to worry about Jasna, the only one of his daughters left in Sarajevo, who lives in the place that the snipers in his building fire at, but after a while he gave up. He hides when they begin to shoot, and he knows she is hiding too. 'I raised all my six girls with good military training,' he says proudly and he shuffles off to show us his medals and talk about the last war, World War II, in which nearly one million Yugoslavs killed each other. Memories of Prozor, 1944, of his wife Nadja, who he says was one of the first Muslim partisan fighters. He says she left Grbavica for health reasons, but Jasna says that her mother could no longer take the fighting and the fear of being a Muslim in a Serb-occupied neighbourhood. Muharem is different. He says he wants to die in his house, that he is not afraid of anything or anyone.

'During the war, I fought with Serbs,' he says. 'Here, I lived with Serbs. No one touched me here. But that war was only a dress rehearsal for this war. This war is bloodier.'

Then he scribbles a note for Jasna in his shaky handwriting:

'*Jasna . . . Dobro sami zdravo iz beograda odavno nemam . . .*' Jasna, I am alright . . . then there is a banging on the door and someone comes in and tells us to leave quickly. I give Muharem some money and he hides it, smiling, says thank you, but Maya tells me after we leave it is almost certain the soldiers will come in, take his letter from Jasna, search the apartment and take his money.

Maya walks me to the end of the town and says goodbye. We kiss and I give her my number in London, which she takes and puts in her pocket. If you need something, I say, but she waves her hand as if to say, who could help us now?

'We cannot live together,' she says. She is not bitter, but there is too much pain. The death of her father, her mother, her neighbours, her friends, a war that has ripped Bosnia apart for 22 months. But Jasna, living in a tall block of flats in Heroes' Square on the other side, where the front line is an abandoned building which runs into a trench, clings to something, an ideal, a belief that things could be the way they were before. 'If they divide the city, it will be like dividing myself,' she says. She does not see, does not want to see the reality. Sarajevo is effectively divided, interpositioned by United Nations troops and sliced into occupied territories: three urban neighbourhoods, and seven municipalities are now held by Serbs. That week in Pale, Radovan Karadzic reiterated his position that Sarajevo can only exist if it is ethnically divided. 'Do you live with a man after he forces you to sleep with him?' Todor Duttina asked me months ago. It is hard now not to agree with him.

But the Bosnians stand to lose the most and so they are firm, resolute that they cannot split the city, that the notion of a Berlin or Nicosia is incomprehensible. They have sustained too many casualties – 10,000 in Sarajevo alone – to give up everything they have fought to defend. 'What we are now witnessing is history in the making,' says Jasna's husband Ilijas, a historian. 'Unfortunately, it is bad history in the making.' The Bosnian government, who have always characterised Sarajevo as multicultural and ethnically tolerant, are adamant that it must remain that way, even if war has turned neighbours into enemies. 'It is not natural to divide a city. Even the Berlin Wall has been dismantled. With the Russians arriving in Sarajevo, the atmosphere has returned to a Cold War, a Yalta atmosphere,' says Senada Kreso, a Bosnian minister. 'For you, the Bridge of Brotherhood and Unity between Grbavica and Hrasno is a joke. For us, it is not. We believe in it.'

Jasna sits inside her flat, thinking. She has also remained in Sarajevo on principle. Two years ago, she watched her two daughters, one twenty-one, one eighteen, drive out on the last safe convoy crossing through Serb lines, travelling, without knowing, through recently 'cleansed' territory. They are now in Munich; she has not seen them since.

Now they are all gone. Her eldest sister, Esreta, the one born in the woods during the last war, crawled across the airport runway last winter, lost her shoes on the barbed wire, and walked across the mountains in the snow, to be reunited with her 24-year-old daughter who was ill with cancer in Moscow. 'When my sister left, she came running back to me and threw me a pack of cigarettes,' Jasna says. 'I said, don't cry, you are going to a better place. But she was crying because she knew she would not return to the same city.'

One by one, the rest of the family disbanded. Sunita, the doctor, escaped through Serbian lines with a false identification card, then got from Belgrade to Italy. Another sister, Azra, got out on a convoy to Belgrade and lives there now, working as a journalist. Their mother, Nadja, seventy, left in November. 'My mother fought against Hitler, but she had to leave Sarajevo,' Jasna says sardonically. She has only spoken to her parents twice in eighteen months, when they phoned her from Grbavica police station. The first time was when Serb soldiers stormed her parents' flat and the line was disconnected. 'I phoned her neighbour to find out news, but I was so frustrated – I could not walk ten minutes away to help my mother.'

But Jasna will not leave. Even when Hrasno was under heavy bombardment, and glass was scattered on the floor of her apartment for weeks, Jasna never gave up the dream that the end of the war would mean a united city. But now, with the United Nations guarding the Bridge of Brotherhood and Unity, she believes the city is splitting in two and she wants to run away like her five sisters, but she is rooted to this place. 'Why did I stay all this time?' she says. 'My sisters left, why didn't I?'

All that week, the city was talking about the end of the war. Is it over? General Sir Michael Rose now strides confidently down Marsala Tito Street, something unthinkable one year ago. The prices on the black market have dropped; the trams will be running soon; there is talk of water returning, and electricity. But Jasna, who is still sitting in the dark, asking me to get a message to her father, is unsure.

'The war is not over,' she says, 'until I can walk to Grbavica and see my father.'

★

Sarajevo, in the words of one journalist, was no longer under siege, but was being tortured. People were still living in a kind of hazy, dream world, drifting through the city as though they were only semi- conscious. I was walking through the snow, picking my way down a hillside coming back from Fatima's house when I saw a tall, spindly figure rushing towards me, calling my name. As he got closer, his features blurred for a moment, I could not recognise him: I saw a beautiful, classical Bosnian face, thin nose, full lips, high cheekbones, and deep-set eyes, a pair of cowboy boots; a fringed cowboy jacket. A teenager with a cigarette dangling out of the corner of his mouth. I stopped and then realising who it was, threw my arms around him.

It was Eldin, a fourteen-year-old boy I had met in the trenches near Stup. He had been introduced to me as one of the youngest soldiers, when I had been spending the spring following soldiers around. Then, he really was a kid: on 1 May 1993, he turned thirteen and there was a birthday party for him. His mother, a sturdy woman who had lost her husband to cancer before the war and her two eldest sons to refugee status, had baked Eldin a war cake made with hoarded rations, no eggs and no flour. The next day we sat on the floor and she showed me photographs of another life: Eldin as a baby, her two eldest sons in their military service uniforms, somewhere in Serbia, her husband at their wedding, dancing, Eldin playing basketball. She made me eat, although I knew it was the only food they had had for maybe a week; homemade bread and some feta cheese from the humanitarian aid package. She was proud of Eldin, but she was terrified: he was on the front line at Stup, there was fighting every day, he was in the trenches, couldn't we talk to the boy and try to make him see some sense?

Eldin, who was learning English, laughed. He had run away at the beginning of the war and had lied about his age to the Armija, talked his way into seeing the Bosnian top soldier Sefer Halilovic, said he wanted to fight. Eventually, they took him on as a runner, later as a soldier. He did not know how to use a gun when he started, now he can strip and clean an automatic weapon and recognise different mortars. I have a mental image of him: this lanky kid, and he really looked like a kid when he was thirteen, all elbows and knees, in a uniform too big, with this wide grin, like an overgrown puppy. I remember him on a bicycle, somebody's bicycle, and his mother standing over him, watching him eat.

I didn't see him for nearly eight months and it was snowing when he stood in front of me, lankier and tall, taller than me, at least six inches taller than when I last saw him. He had been sledding and there was snow in his soft brown hair and snow melting on his eyelashes.

He told me then that his mother had died, been killed the week before by a mortar shell that ripped through the kitchen. He had come back from the trenches and she was washing his uniform ... he stopped and lit another cigarette. He's chain-smoking, I thought, when did he start chain-smoking?

When I looked down my hands were balled up into little mitts. I said, 'Oh Eldin, I'm so so sorry,' thinking, he is only a kid, and now he is alone. He said his uncle was looking after him, but please, could I help him get to Sweden? There was nothing in Sarajevo for him anymore.

I put my hand on his back and we walked back to town, him smoking, and got into the black VW and drove to Bambus, a restaurant that served watery pizza made from humanitarian aid for 30 DM. I bought him one, but he did not talk the entire time he ate, and it took him longer than anyone else to finish.

Later he told me how she died: she was washing his uniform, he said, leaning over the sink, and he was sitting on the sofa a few feet away, with his feet up on the table, but he can't remember what they were talking about. A shell fell next door; it happened so quickly that he cannot quite remember except that something hit her in the throat and she dropped to the floor holding her neck and died very quickly, even before the neighbours ran in. He was screaming, he did not know if he had been hit, but he knew enough about corpses to know that she was dead. He had been protected by the wall that he was sitting against.

Now he moved like a zombie. Fourteen years old and what had he seen? He asked me again to please get him out; you know I have a brother in Sweden, he said. I knew because I had seen the photographs that his mother had shown me, one beautiful spring day, one year ago. There was nothing left for him in Sarajevo, and besides, if he didn't get out of this city that had taken everything from him, mother, father, aunts, uncles, he was going to go mad. His eyes were enormous.

We met for coffee again the next day, and I introduced him to a Swedish journalist and I made some calls, but then I had to go back to London. When I came back to Sarajevo six weeks later, it was spring and I went looking for him, it was close to the time of his birthday and I wanted to do something for him, because he really was still a kid. But he was gone. Someone said he went to Sweden, he had got out with the Red Cross. Someone else said he had gone to Zagreb. His uncle who had been living in the flat that I had sat in with his mother was gone, the door was locked. The ping-pong table that we had played on the summer before was still there, but the dog that lived next door had also disappeared.

In February 1994, I walked to Zlata's house, and when I reached the bridge that Alma, a Bosnian friend, and I used to run across, holding hands and pulling each other so that we could move faster, I walked. Everything had happened, and now you could walk down the street and even near the river without waiting for the bullet.

Zlata's flat was empty because she was gone. She was in London in fact that week, giving a press conference to launch her book, a thirteen-year-old superstar who had begun writing a diary and had suddenly spiralled into a symbol. She was sitting on a platform flanked by her mother and her father, both of them nervous and slightly baffled to be in the middle of a press conference.

'What do you want to be when you grow up?' I said one afternoon, sitting in her bedroom covered with pictures of Linda Evangelista and Claudia Schiffer. 'Think hard. Don't say, if I ever grow up, because you know you will.'

Her brow furrowed. 'You know – a journalist.'

I laughed and hugged the pillow that was on my lap. 'No, come on, really. A journalist? After Sarajevo? What do you really want to do?'

But she was serious. 'It's interesting,' she said. 'To be a journalist. Don't you think?'

Zlata was the same age as Eldin, but they did not know each other. Both were self-possessed and both had grown up during the war. I once wrote of Zlata that she had the kind of confidence that maybe comes with growing up well-off, slightly spoiled, with intelligent parents who lavish you with praise and believe that you are wonderful. But she was also brave and had managed to work out a system when it came to the war: how not to be afraid, how to stay strong for her parents.

Alicia, her mother, was thin and delicate with long straight blonde hair. She had lost a baby once when Zlata was tiny, and so she treasured her thirteen-year-old who played Chopin dutifully on the piano, who could recite poetry, who could dance and rollerskate. Alicia was a chemist before the war, working for a major corporation; now she was working for the city, testing the water supply. She had suffered terribly during the siege: perhaps it was harder on the people who had been well-off before the war. To rely on packages for food, to stand in a queue for water, to have to apologise when guests come to visit and they cannot use the lavatory because there is no water in the cistern. And no coffee to offer, no sugar, no drinks.

The apartment was the same apartment that she had lived in with her husband, a lawyer, since she was married twenty years ago. It was airy, spacious, with a Viennese feel: huge sash windows, now blown out and replaced by plastic, a piano in the bedroom, now the one safe room and sandbags everywhere.

They had lost a lot: friends, their weekend house in the hills above Sarajevo, books, clothes, their money. Alicia was so thin that she appeared breakable, so slight and pale that her daughter, who had actually grown during the war, appeared robust beside her.

There was one day in October 1993 that I will never forget. All week, I had been working on a feature story about the trams, about the return of normal life in Sarajevo. As I sat in Vesna's kitchen on Sunday morning, her brother Nino said that the day he heard the tram bell was the day he would believe the war was over, and he was laughing, saying no, Janine, that day is not here yet, no way.

'The day I take these sandbags down,' he said, 'is the day the war is over.' Everyone had their own prerequisite for the end: when I can water my garden, when I can drive to Ilidza, when I can pick up the telephone and call my son in Berlin, when my children come back to me.

Zlata's was different: 'When the shelling stops,' she said. And on that October day, one of the worst days, when the shelling began at 5 am for no reason that anyone can think of, I reached their house and they had been underground for hours. Alicia was shaking and crying, practically retching with grief and sorrow. We sat upstairs and she shook so hard her foot was tapping on the wooden floor. Oh my God, no more, no more. Zlata was sitting behind her, solemn but composed.

'Are you okay?' I said, and she replied in a small voice, so eerie to hear it coming from a child:

'I have to be okay.'

★

So the war is effectively over, but time is standing still, frozen on the last day of normality, April 1992. Who could remember any kind of life before? And would it ever be possible to forget what had happened?

I still think it was hardest for the younger children, because they were too young to understand. The older ones had a sense that something terrible was happening outside – that these things called *grenatas* landed on the pavement and splintered into a million pieces of flying steel and burned their way through your skin, and pierced your body, and then you died. Some of them knew that they could never walk in the street again, because there was someone in the hills looking down, like a monster standing over a doll's house with an open hand. Some of them had lost their parents, some of them lost their friends, some of them lost legs, arms, eyes, chunks of their faces gouged out by a sniper bullet. There was one fourteen-year-old girl, beautiful, with long hair and a strong, supple body, a prizewinning swimmer. Every day, before the war, she would train in the Olympic swimming pool, doing her laps, her freestyle, practising her butterfly. She was running through the streets one day when a shell landed and she was far enough away from it to live, but close enough to lose one of her breasts and part of her lung.

After she was released from hospital, she told her mother it was a good thing it was wartime, because she wouldn't have been able to practise anyway, they had drained all the swimming pools at the start.

Some of them grew up, losing all sense of innocence in a very short time. Nusret Krasnic, who was nine when I first met him, and lived in Ljubica Ivezic orphanage on Bjelave, opposite Klea's house, tended to live as though there was no sense of time. He knew what war was, because his mother was killed in front of him when a shell fell on their kitchen. He knew about *grenatas*, because he lay in his bed – a pile of clothes in a corner – in the dark. He knew about snipers because he had been pinned down inside a flowerpot on the bridge crossing the Mijelka for hours. He did not know how long he had been in the orphanage; he thought maybe a month, two months? But the director of the place, a sinister-looking man, said that Nusret had been there for one year.

The orphanage was probably the worst place, aside from the morgue, in Sarajevo. It was Dickensian, dank, smelled of sour boiled food although there was hardly any food at all in the filthy kitchen, only rice, strawberry yoghurt powder and beans, twice a day. It also smelled of damp. There were rats, cold, wet, oily floors and rain poured in the open windows which had been blown out by the impact of the shells. There were no toilets; the children rarely washed and their hair was matted with dirt. They slept eight or nine to a room; some had beds, others had sleeping bags piled in a corner. They wore ripped t-shirts even in the coldest weather. Nusret wore socks on his hands instead of mittens. I hated going there, because when you walked in the door, you were immediately surrounded by a pack of hungry, crawling kids who pulled your hair, went through your pockets, your bags, demanded cigarettes, chocolates, food. They shouted at you: 'Fuck you, bitch!' 'Welcome to Hell!' 'Fuck you, fuck you, you bitch!' and 'Give me a cigarette, fuck you!'

They jumped on the back of humanitarian aid trucks and stole food; they sniffed glue when they could get it. Most of them were mentally retarded, the ones who were not appeared to be slowly going mad.

The routine goes like this: every morning when he wakes up, Nusret crawls out of the pile of clothes under which he sleeps and thinks about one thing: how to get home. The house in Sirokaca Street where he lived with his parents and two brothers is now demolished, a pile of rubble on the front line, but at least once a week Nusret leaves the orphanage, climbing out of a window because he is usually locked into his room by the shrewish refugee woman who looks after him, and tries to get home. Sometimes he makes it as far as his old neighbourhood, often he is caught in the shooting and shelling, and some nights he is unable to get back to Bjelave because he has been caught in the fighting. One night, he slept in the basement of an abandoned hotel, curled up in a ball like an animal for warmth.

He is more like an animal than a child, really: a small boy, barely three feet high, his skin mottled by the cold, his teeth sharp like a woodland animal and chipped. He's running through the snow in a pair of boots that someone gave him, too big, with a dog called Juju who lives in the orphanage and with whom he sleeps, and he's slightly off balance, running with a limp. He goes sledding by holding onto the back of humanitarian aid trucks in the street.

He's shy; he doesn't like to talk very much, has, in fact, stopped talking much since he got to the orphanage. When he talks about his mother, Ljubica, who was killed by a shell in front of him, it's not about her, but about food and memories of eating: the smell of potato pie, or *burek*, the Bosnian pastry stuffed with meat or cheese, or just the smell of meat – something he finds hard to describe – drifting through from the kitchen. Once, there were presents of chocolate and nuts and oranges.

Ljubica died in the kitchen in May 1992, at night, standing by the sink. It was a mundane way to die: maybe she was getting a glass of water, having got out of bed, maybe she was concerned about the shelling that was getting too close to the house, maybe she couldn't sleep and was thinking of her husband, fighting somewhere in the hills behind the house. Nusret, who was lying in bed at the time with his fourteen-year-old brother Muhammed, seems to remember that she was washing dishes, because he could hear the water running, the sound of splashing and her voice singing in the kitchen. Then she stopped singing and everything went deadly quiet in that way it does for a few seconds when a shell lands – it came through the roof and for a short time, although it seemed to him like hours, there was that quiet and then the chaos: the confusion of the neighbours screaming, walls collapsing, windows breaking, the sound of glass scattering, people rushing in and out of his house, men storming inside, taking her body. Muhammed stood beside him, they watched the doctors taking her away and they tried to follow her out of the house. Someone stopped him, made him get dressed and he and Muhammed were sent next door to sleep at a neighbour's.

The neighbours who were looking after the two boys didn't have enough humanitarian aid to feed all of them, so after a week they brought them to the Hotel Europa. The Europa was a festering hole in the centre of Sarajevo, once one of the grandest hotels in the Balkans, a refugee centre now, swarming with people living in dark, wet corners, standing in lines waiting to be given a pair of plastic boots from the Red Cross. Before they left them, the neighbours told them that their father had been killed, and that night, in a corner of the basement, they made a vow with each other: they would look after themselves, and they would live on the streets.

Being in the Hotel Europa, which had been targeted and hit by Serb shells, was like being down deep in the 59th Circle. The floorboards would creak under the weight of the refugees, and the kids running through the rooms screamed like maniacs. Some of the luckier families, the first refugees bombarded out of their houses, got to settle in the old hotel rooms, gutted with no windows, but with room to sleep on the floor. An older refugee woman took the two boys and tried to watch them, tried to fight in the line and get some food for them, but in a place like that it is difficult enough just to fight for your own survival. And so, after two months, she walked them down Marsala Tito Street, across the intersection that leads up to General Morillon's residence, and brought them to the orphanage. The problem was, she said, that Nusret kept running away at night, back to his home. He still thought his mother was alive, standing in the same place in the kitchen, singing.

Then there were three of them in the gang, banding together because otherwise you got the shit kicked out of you by the older boys, some of them big kids, but deranged, with wild eyes and big hands who would tie the smaller children up, and steal their food. There were 170 children, most of them war orphans, no more than 20 staff to look after them. Before the war, there had been 52 staff.

When I first met Nusret, it was freezing cold and there was no electricity, of course, no heat, and only one wood stove that the children fought over. Just walking through the cold rooms, or sitting with the director made your bones ache with cold; made the back of your legs stiff when they hit the cold wooden chair. The only room that was warm was the one reserved for the babies, which was always kept locked.

'Why locked?' I asked a young girl, a refugee from eastern Bosnia, who sat with the babies, holding them one at a time, feeding them with the one bottle of humanitarian powdered milk. It was locked to keep the other children out of the one warm room. They stank, those babies, because there was no water to wash them and not enough to staff to change their diapers. One of them, just a few weeks old, was rumoured to be the child of a woman who had been held in a Serbian camp and repeatedly raped; another baby had the same name as me in Serbo-Croat, Janana. I would hold her and afterwards the refugee girl would beg me not to anymore because the baby cried for too long when I had gone.

By that winter, the psychiatrists were already beginning to examine the effects of the war. There were, for instance, by mid-March 1993, 2,000 children killed and more than 10,000 wounded in Sarajevo alone. One paediatrician who worked for the Children's Embassy opposite the Holiday Inn was bitter. 'I don't know what they call those people on the hills who aim their guns at children,' she said. 'They are evil.' She had a file stuffed with stories: the seventeen-year-old boy who lost his testicles; the four-year-old who could not remember an egg. 'They act like little adults,' she said. 'But they lack tenderness and they are frightened even of the smallest sounds – when you drop something, they jump.'

Nusret didn't jump anymore; I thought that was more frightening that watching, for instance, Klea's son Deni, who screamed whenever the shooting began. Nusret's eyes were blank; he stared straight ahead. The war meant something entirely different to him; because he had lost everything, his life had absolutely no context. His friend Dragona, a twenty-year-old who had been in the orphanage for twelve years, explained what war meant: 'It means, for a lot of them, they can do whatever they want,' she said. 'They don't have lessons anymore.

They are bored. They steal because they are allowed to do whatever they want and because they operate like a gang.'

There were no lessons, the school nearby that used to take them was too dangerous for them to get to. Nusret had forgotten how to write his name.

By the spring of 1994, the war had been going on for 24 months, eight seasons, two winters, two springs and two summers. There were some weddings that spring, and another NATO ultimatum, and this time there actually were some perfunctory air strikes around Gorazde to slap Serb hands for everything they had done. But a few weeks later, the story faded again onto the back pages.

I got letters from Mario Susko, now in New York. He was unhappy, desperate, he wanted to go home. Klea and Deni, whom I had held in my arms on his baptism, promising that I would look after him, were lost somewhere in Hercegovina. The number Mario had given me was disconnected. Zoran, Klea's husband, had tried to escape Sarajevo several times unsuccessfully. Because he was a Croat and had served in the HVO in the city, he was having problems with the Armija. The last time I saw him, he was trying to get out through an underground tunnel.

Mario said he was in a prison in Serbia, that he had been captured on the other side at a Serb checkpoint. Klea was out of her mind with grief, wouldn't leave Hercegovina until they were together.

'I never wanted to be a refugee,' Mario said gloomily.

'But you're safe . . . you're alive, come on Mario, you wanted to go, you might have been dead by now. At least you're together and you're alive.'

He paused. 'I'm honestly not being dramatic,' he said. 'But I'm not alive. Not anymore.'

In Sarajevo, they were still trying to open the Bridge of Brotherhood and Unity, across the river that split the Serb side from the other, separating Jasna and Muharem, mothers from fathers, sisters from brothers. When it was eventually opened, it was under strict UN control.

THE JOURNEY

In the beginning, it was easy but strange to leave Bosnia. There was the flight, the Hercules C-130, Maybe Airlines the Norwegian UN soldiers called it because maybe you got there and maybe you didn't, and two or three days in Split, going to the sea or eating shellfish outside. Spending twenty, thirty minutes in the shower; delivering letters; going to the market near the ruins of the old Palace and staring at the flowers: sunflowers, daisies, roses. Then the thought that soon you would be home, able to lie in bed, or use a telephone, buy a newspaper. There was a life outside Bosnia.

But even in Split, you could not really escape, because back at the Hotel Split, the refugees crammed into dormitory-like spaces, living three and four to a room, their dark washing hanging over the balcony of the hotel, could stare straight into your room as you walked out on the balcony, or lay on your bed watching CNN. At dinner, they crowded into the dining room, next to the EC monitors in their white outfits, clutching small tin pots which would be filled with rice, or soup, and which they would carry back to their rooms. They had been there for too long, and they had the look of caged animals. At first a month, then two, then three, now it has been two years since I first went to Split and they are still there, the old men in black sitting on the opposite side of the bar staring at nothing.

The alternative to Maybe Airlines was to drive out of Bosnia:

through the hills, the mountain passes, through the Sarajevo checkpoints, Sierra One, the old Ilidja Serb 'custom point' where a Serb guard once took me to an upstairs room and finding inside one of my socks my stash of money that the managing editor at the *Sunday Times* had given me, relieved me of it for the cause of Greater Serbia. That was in March 1993, and I had been on my way to Tuzla to report on the flow of refugees streaming out of Srebrenica. I had ten hours of mountain road ahead, no car and no money.

'You can't do this to me,' I had said earlier when the Serb commander had interrogated me, counting my Deutschmarks out in neat piles.

'We can do anything we want,' he replied smugly, his oily face leering at me across the desk. 'We're the police.' Later, I heard them laughing.

They told me I could get my money back in Belgrade after the war, and gave me a receipt. It was the same receipt they gave the Muslims and Croats after they flushed them out of their villages, the same paper they presented when they relieved them of their houses, their cars, their possessions. I sat on a kerb and wept, but it was only money, I wasn't raped, and it wasn't even my money. I realised then for the first time that what I was feeling, humiliation, frustration, rage, was nothing, could not even begin to compare with what the Bosnians had endured.

There was a Serb soldier there that day, a kind one, whom I would see repeatedly over the next year. He had what my mother would call a good face: kind, intelligent, sensitive. He knew what had happened to me and my two friends inside the checkpoint, how we had been robbed, and he also knew what was happening inside Sarajevo, a few kilometres down the road. He couldn't speak any English, but he gave me a cigarette and a paper napkin and shook his head. Don't cry, it's alright, it's the war. He sat with me and said nothing, but I believed that he felt embarrassed and ashamed.

The rest of that drive meant passing through Vitez, the British forward base, and Prozor, the town where I had seen a dead donkey lying in the middle of the road and Muslim civilians crying in terror, running in their bedroom slippers after the Croats had cleansed them from their village. And then Tomislavgrad, where the Jajce refugees were held, or if you went the other way, the old Mostar road if it was still open, where the journey could be so ominous and strange that the hair stood on the back of our necks as we drove ('If I'm ever gonna get it,' one photographer friend always said to me, 'it's going to be on the Mostar road. It's bad karma.') and finally over the border into Croatia, where the police in dark Ray-Bans made you clear out of the car and searched the back just to be obnoxious, and then the open road to Split.

I can't forget those trips even if I want to, even if the details blur – the time my Lada Niva broke down and my interpreter and I had to practically push it every time it stalled; the time I drove towards Vitez with David Mills in an armoured car and we got stuck in the mud and I had to hitchhike back to Split to get a tow truck. Those stories, those events are not buried. They are all somewhere in thirty, forty, fifty little green notebooks hidden in the back of my cupboard, along with the letters, the papers, the notes, so that I know I can never forget any of it.

The North Vietnamese writer Bao Ninh spent ten years turning his experiences of war into a novel. He was one of ten fighters who survived from a youth brigade of 500 and it took him ten years to remember it all. What he wrote about was grief, loss and death. But he also wrote about love: what it was like to be seventeen, that pure, that innocent. War ended it all, the day his battalion was spray-gunned by American helicopters and most of his friends, the people he had played cards with hours before, died. He ends the novel, *The Sorrow of War*, with this:

> Those were the days when all of us were very young, very pure and very sincere.

I do not know if that kind of innocence and purity pertains to Sarajevo, but I have my own interpretation, because I know that something great was lost; certainly those soldiers who left school and went to Otes or Zuc or Trebevic are never going to be able to go back to that old life, the cafés, the football, the lovers, without remembering someone who was killed next to them. Eldin, Zlata, Irma, Mario, Zoran, Vesna ... will any of them forget?

If you are being destroyed and you feel as though the world does not know, worse, does not care, how do you begin to live your life again when it suddenly becomes normal?

★

Two years after the war began, something's happened in Sarajevo: there are traffic lights, gifts of the Austrian government someone tells me, and books for sale in the market. My friend Renzo Cianfanelli gives me a present: a *Private Eye* cartoon book. 'Just to amuse you,' he says. There are people in the streets and the telephones are ringing. Trams are running down Snipers' Alley, you can ride them for free; the price of pizza has gone down. One day, to my amazement, I walk into the Holiday Inn and see my old friends, the waiters, opening the new restaurant. We hug each other like old friends, and they are proud that they have a normal restaurant now in a place that used to be too dangerous to walk by.

But even though the war is over, the emotional impact is beginning to hit hard. Dina, the Bosnian BBC assistant producer who had had to put up with journalists rushing into her office complaining because no one was getting killed, was sitting drinking tea with me when she started laughing.

'Don't you miss the old days?'

We both laughed because we knew they weren't the good old days, but there was a kind of emotional bond that drew everything together: the wind tunnel sucking in the past, pulling it back again.

Back to Sarajevo, June 1994. On the Hercules going back to Split, I'm sitting in the airport, perched on top of my black duffle bag, the one I always use, and out of nowhere I see a face laughing, filled with a mixture of sorrow and happiness. It is Boyan Hadzihalilovic, one of Sarajevo's most talented artists who, with his wife Dada, designed the posters that were to become the symbols of the war. Years ago, before the war, they were so good that they won a Saatchi and Saatchi Big Ideas Award, but trapped in Sarajevo without supplies, they forgot that there was anything else besides the war.

'At the beginning, we were shocked and scared,' he says. 'But ten days after the war started, we began to make the posters in impossible conditions. We had to, you know, to do something for the town.'

They're leaving the city, finally, after two years inside. It's the first time that they could get out, and they are overcome with emotion: 'How many times did we try to escape?' he says to me, and I remember the winter before last when he and Dada tried night after night to cross the airport road, dressed in their warmest clothing taking only one bag, their art supplies. They were going to Zenica, in Central Bosnia, where someone had offered them a space to work ('with some electricity!' Dada had said at the time, like a child, because in the longest days of winter they would work in their apartment without anything). Every time they reached the strategic point on the airport road where they might or might not be able to leave Sarajevo for ever, they were turned back by the UN. And the next night, they would try again.

So they ended up staying, they ended up getting married in Sarajevo, during the height of the war in January 1993. Boyan wore a tuxedo, far too big, and sneakers; Dada had a borrowed dress. They lived in a kind of commune, nine people in two large apartments, opposite the Presidency building; Dada and Boyan in one apartment, Boyan's sister Nadja, whom I knew well, with her husband in another, their parents on the top floor, and various friends and wounded relations staying wherever there was a spare bed. 'You know, there are streets in this town I haven't been to in more than a year?' Boyan said to me one day. Before the war, his father owned one of the most prestigious art galleries in Sarajevo; he lost it and most of the paintings during the bombardment.

But Dada and Boyan had stayed throughout, producing the posters. He's got them now, along with one suitcase, the only thing they are taking with them, and a borrowed flak jacket because you need one to get on a United Nations flight. We're hugging in the gloomy waiting-room of Sarajevo airport, and a woman with a booming American accent comes up and says, 'Are you the two that did these posters? I've been looking for you for eight months.'

'Yes, we are,' Boyan says and because she wants them autographed, he does it patiently, and Dada and I are laughing, because we're remembering all of those days, those nights, scrounging for cigarettes in one room in their apartment, the only safe room, and the other rooms sealed with all the furniture pushed against the windows. And the *burek*, the pastry, that their mother made for parties, even though they had hardly enough for all of them, the best parties in Sarajevo, everyone went, and suddenly we're standing in the airport.

'The first time in two years,' Boyan says, 'that I have left Sarajevo.'

The flight takes forty minutes, that amazing flight across Central Bosnia, where the streams and rivers look like they're cut out of the mountains, and the roads jutting out and then, the Adriatic. We land and unstrap and rip the flak jackets off and Dada and Boyan are standing back, like two kids, not quite knowing what you expect when you have been inside a place for two years, really not two years: a lifetime.

We get outside the plane. We are in Split, on the coast, in Croatia. Bosnia, Sarajevo, the airport, Snipers' Alley, the flat near the Presidency, is a lifetime ago. Boyan says, 'You can't imagine what this means to us, you can't know how it feels,' and as we're walking towards the Croatian passport control, Dada is crying, or is she smiling? I can't tell, but we lean together and then she is laughing.

'For the first time in two years,' she says, her eyes closing against the breeze, and she's got tears in her eyes, one for joy, one for sorrow, 'I can smell the sea.'

GLOSSARY OF
ABBREVIATIONS

NATO	North Atlantic Treaty Organisation
DM	Deutschmark
UN	United Nations
UNHCR	United Nations High Commission for Refugees
UNPROFOR	United Nations forces in the former Yugoslavia
HVO	Croat Defence Council
SDS	Serbian Democratic Party in Bosnia
CARE	Co-operative for American Relief to Everywhere
JNA	Yugoslav National Army
ICRC	International Committee of the Red Cross
WHO	World Health Organisation